Wicca Starter Kit

Candles, Herbs, Tarot Cards, Crystals, and Spells. A Beginner's Guide to Using the Fundamental Elements of Wiccan Rituals (2022 Crash Course for Newbies)

Ava Walton

Table of Contents

Introduction

Wicca Starter Kit is your comprehensive guide to casting spells and performing rituals, complete with all of the instruments you'll need to bring nature's and the divine's power into your life. When you work as a solitary practitioner, you control the rituals, the equipment you employ, and the types of spells you construct to accomplish your magical rites. Finding all of the necessary tools can be difficult, but having a good resource guide to help you get started can make all the difference.

Whether you are new to Wicca or have been practicing for a long, this book will provide you with an overview and introduction to the history of Wicca, the concepts underlying its philosophies, and some of the reasons for celebrating this lovely magic. It is critical to have the background to grasp the tools and reasons for your work.

The most crucial aspect of the Wicca Starter Kit is your guidance on the tools you'll need to execute rituals and spells. In Chapter 2, you will find a concise list of magical implements to assist you to explore your Wicca practice, as well as an explanation of what they are used for, how to use them, when to use them, and where to find them for your altar and practice.

The Wicca Starter Kit will also include several chapters of step-by-step instructions for constructing and honoring your altar space.

Casting a magical circle, performing rituals, and composing and casting spells are all examples of witchcraft. There is also a chapter dedicated to the use of crystal magic and another to candle magic.

Overall, Wicca Starter Kit is an excellent resource for getting started with rituals and spells using some of the most common instruments in the field. Whatever you see on these pages is certain to increase your understanding of your craft and assist you in moving forward on So mote it be!

Chapter 1

Introduction to Wicca,

A Brief History of Wicca

Welcome to Wicca's brief history! As you learn more about the mysteries and enchantment of this magnificent craft, it will be crucial for you to understand where it came from. Many Wiccan traditions are derived from more ancient Pagan belief systems and rituals; however, the emergence of Wicca and its founding beliefs started in England and was presented in the mid-1950s by a British civil servant named Gerald Gardner.

Wicca is classified as Neo-Paganism by some, yet it has specific elements and characteristics that distinguish it from the conventional varieties of paganism practiced in more ancient societies.

Before Gardner's public introduction of Wicca in 1954, the concepts of Wicca could be traced back to Margaret Murray, a renowned folklorist, anthropologist, and Egyptologist who studied the traditions and cultures of a wide range of religious practices, combining a field study of these sects and describing the concept of witchcraft in her own words.

Murray wrote several publications regarding medieval religious practices, particularly witch cults in Europe. Her publications motivated readers to reignite the pagan arts by forming their covens and basing their worship on Murray's descriptions. All of this was going on in the early 1920s in the United Kingdom and Europe, and it most likely led to Gerald Gardner's more structured worldview known as Wicca.

Gardener's book, Witchcraft Today, explained the origins of the term Wicca and what it means in the context of the craft. In his work, it is spelled with only one 'c,' as in "which," and the second 'c' was not added until the 1960s. Gardner notes that 'which' is a Gaelic or Scots-English word that means "intelligent people." He had always had a fascination with the occult, and eventually

In the late 1930s, he was initiated into his coven. In the late 1940s, he founded his coven, purchasing land and using it as a center for folklore research. It became his occult headquarters, where he would bring the Wiccan way to light through his books and practice.

Gardner had a close relationship with the renowned occultist Alister Crowley. When the two men met in the late 1940s, they had a lot to talk about regarding their personal views and magic. Gardner's work, as well as his writing out of his Wiccan rites for publication, were heavily affected by Crowley's work, which extended back to the early part of the century.

Gardner published his works, including a novel titled High Magic's Aid, which became one of his first standard tomes to define Wicca practice. However, it was his Book of Shadows that became the most well-known and sought-after.

Gardner's Book of Shadows was his collection of spells, rituals, and other occult literature. It is still one of the most important books for practicing Wicca or at least learning from the original Wiccan, Gardner himself. Fortunately, Wicca was and still is an ever-evolving discipline that does not follow a precise set of principles. It is a very adaptable religion that encourages individuals to follow a simple set of beliefs and concepts while also allowing them to explore and gain a better grasp of those ideals.

Gardner's coven initiates were handed the Book of Shadows to copy and use as one of the ways they belonged to the coven, sharing the same spells and rituals to carry on and practice.

Gardner met Doreen Valientes in the early 1950s before Wicca became popular. She called him after reading an article in a magazine about covens, witches, their customs, and what life was like for them. She was able to edit The Book of Shadows under Gardner's supervision for Gardner to market it as a popular book for children.

Others outside of the coven, as well as notable Wiccan circles, were sold in the same way Crowley had marketed his beliefs and conclusions.

Valientes rose to prominence as a Wiccan coven leader and scholar in the rapidly rising Wiccan community.

When viewed in this light, the narrative of Wicca appears to be nothing more than a footnote in the annals of history, yet when examined further, it had a tremendous impact on the realm of magic. Before Gardner introduced his new religion, there were various ways for people to pursue the ancient Pagan arts.

Witchcraft was an extremely forbidden practice that was frowned upon for generations following the witch trials.

Margaret Murray's study of the past helped people gain a fresh appreciation and understanding of the beauty of ancient magic, and Wicca might not have existed if it hadn't been for her work and that of other occult philosophers.

To be honest, it has always existed in some form or another, and it has gone by many different names. Pagan is a broad umbrella term that encompasses a wide range of different sects and denominations, rites, and rituals.

So, it begs the question, what distinguishes Wicca?

Modern-day Wicca approaches connection to the divine through rituals and practices, solstice festivals, observances of deities, notably a male and female god form, herbalism, a code of ethics, and a belief in reincarnation and an afterlife.

Some argue that it is a modern interpretation of pagan faiths and rituals that existed before Christianity. It has European beginnings, but in today's world, it will combine principles from various religious practices such as Shamanism and pre-Christian Egyptian religion. It has also been highlighted that there are striking similarities to Druidism, despite the paucity of information about how the Druids genuinely worshipped.

The majority of Wiccans worship a male god and a female goddess, or the Horned God and Mother Goddess, or Mother Earth. It is not always the case, and even in Gardner's day, early variants of Wicca were not strictly adhered to. Most of the time, what deities would be worshipped by the group and how specific rituals would be performed were decided coven by the coven.

Other Wiccan practices include, but are not limited to, atheism, pantheism, and polytheism. This leveled the playing field for anyone desiring to develop a Wiccan practice, incorporating all of the other ethics and rituals into their work while having the freedom to worship however they see fit. The fundamentals stay constant, but the deities or objects of worship change.

Apart from the elements stated in the earliest forms of Wicca, there is a deep respect for the Earth and all of its inhabitants, which is why Wicca is sometimes referred to as a nature-based religion. The use of herbs and plants in spell work and rituals is regularly acknowledged, as is a commitment to the seasons of the Earth cycles and Moon cycles, giving attention to all living rhythms.

Wicca's history may appear to be recent, yet it stems from a long and green history of pagans, druids, witches, warlocks, and all of the individuals and covens who had a real devotion to the presence of Earth magic and all of its gifts. Giving attention to the beginnings of Wicca is a crucial starting point for your research, and as you embrace the techniques of how Wicca can be practiced, like many who came before you, you can expand on it to make it work for you in the way that feels best. There are merely guidelines and no hard and fast regulations. Wicca is intended to change with the individual, and whether you practice alone or with others, the Wicca of the past will always be a part of the Wicca of the present. Your witchcraft.

The following chapter will delve deeper into some of the key ideas and principles of all branches of Wicca to assist you in determining you're safe to practice.

Wicca's Fundamental Beliefs and Philosophies

Wicca can be regarded as a broad religion since it embraces a wide range of perspectives, realities, and beliefs. There are, however, three fundamental core principles that the majority of Wiccans practice to provide a solid foundation for comprehending the magic you are working with when practicing.

These ideas are considered regardless of whatever coven you belong to or whose deity you worship. The ideas presented in this chapter provide the basic platform, or basis, of what Wicca is and how it explains itself to anyone interested in following this path.

Nature is a Divine Being.

The majority of Wiccans believe that nature is divine. It serves as the practice's backbone, and there are numerous ways in which this core concept reveals itself in various rituals. Every rock, tree, leaf, plant, animal, bird, bug, and person, not to mention hundreds of thousands of additional species and landscapes, are all members of this Earth.

Our sacred home is the Earth, and we are a precious part of it. All life energy is stored and reproduced there, and we are a part of those cycles and processes. Worshiping nature is worshipping the core of all things. And you will discover that all Wiccan holidays and festivals are derived from nature worship.

A solstice or equinox marks each holiday. The lunar cycle determines all esbats. And almost every ingredient in these rituals and spells derives from nature in some way.

In nature, there is also a celebration of the oneness of opposing forces.

There is always a balance of light and dark in nature, and worship allows us to see life from that perspective serenity and balance are the presence of male and female in everything; yin and yang. That is how nature works.

The practice of devoting space and love to nature is part of the Wiccan belief, and while it is not required, it is recommended.

When you consider all of the other key ideas, that practice follows naturally.

Many of the tools you'll need for your rituals and spells come from nature. You'll find yourself gathering herbs or wood pieces to make a wand. You could be gathering plants to decorate your home for a certain event, or you could be adorning your altar with scents and treasures from the forest floor. Wicca incorporates everything from nature, and it is a strong technique to truly connect with the divine in nature.

Reincarnation, Karma, and the Afterlife

Karma is an echo of the Threefold Law (see below), which simply argues that what you do in one life carries over into the next. To make such a recommendation, one must believe in the notion of reincarnation, which opens the door for your spiritual being and essence to return to another life after your last one to continue learning lessons and acquiring knowledge for the progress of all things.

According to Wicca, this is what will always be and has always been, and therefore to adopt Wicca's principles, you must examine the reality of who you were before and who you will be next. It's possible that you're already familiar with some of your former life experiences and knows what lessons you're attempting to acquire from them. In other circumstances, you learn new things as you go and aren't necessarily aware of what you're supposed to be learning. The concept of Karma encourages you to remember what you need to heal from your previous life to climb further into your actual power and magic. And, while you're doing it, make sure that what you do in this life is something you want to carry with you into the next. This also applies to the Wiccan Rede of "hurt none" (see below).

Although there is the concept of reincarnation, there is also the concept of the afterlife, sometimes known as Summerland, where you rest between incarnations to prepare for the next one.

To design the best path forward, gather your strength and reflect on your previous adventure.

All of these ideas assist the Wiccan in bridging the gap between Earth and Spirit and ensuring that the divine balance is always present, no matter what life you are living or what stage of travel you are in between worlds.

Ancestors

In the practice of Wiccan rituals and casting, it is usual to invoke the ancestors. Many Wiccans think that our ancestors are always with us, guiding us and teaching us the way and that they should be revered for their dedication to moving forward and living life.

Wiccans respect numerous deities, and it is natural to incorporate your ancestors into your practice regularly, as they are a part of the cycle of the self and have many lessons to teach you as you grow and honor your path. The concept of respecting the ancestors is not exclusive to Wicca; it is a universal reality found in most religious practices.

A great deal of ancestor worship stems from a desire to appreciate both the past and what your ancestors continue to do for you in the future.

The Year's Wheel

In Wicca, all of the yearly cycles are celebrated. Every solstice, as well as every equinox, has a celebration, or Sabbat. The rituals and spells associated with these periods are sacred honoring and celebrations dedicated to the end of something to herald the advent of something new. Some innumerable deaths and rebirths can occur in the calendar of the year, and as a Wiccan, you will discover peace and abundance with each passing season because of that very truth: life begets death, which begets more life.

There are moon cycles in each season that are commemorated during the Esbat ceremony. The moon's cycles order the seasons, and every declining moon heralds the end of something.

Every waxing moon leads to a tremendous fullness, which has its magic and ritual associated with it.

All of the rhythms and cycles are a part of Wiccan labor and will remain for the rest of the time. Worshiping the divine in nature is strongly related to the wheel of the year and should be considered an important component of Wiccan worship.

Personal accountability and accountability

This idea is consistent with the Wiccan Rede and the Threefold Law.

Every action you take is your responsibility. Wicca demands that you be mindful of your power, since it may be greater than you think, especially when interacting with the sacred divine energies of all things and all life.

When you practice Wicca, you become accountable for more than just yourself; you use the energy of all life to celebrate and support the life you lead, and anything you do can affect someone else. It is also a good opportunity for you to be honest with yourself about the fact of karma because anything you are responsible for in this life follows you into the next.

You are extremely powerful, and Wicca assists you in embracing your inherent power and life force energy; nevertheless, it also requires you to be responsible with your power, to hurt none, and to do right by your acts and rituals.

The Wiccan Rede: Do No Harm

The Wiccan Rede simply states that you should not do anything in your practice that could damage another person. The primary premise of the golden rule of thumb is to do unto others as you would have them do unto you, but it also asks you to be very cautious in your practice and to examine how you frame your spells and rituals.

Wicca's practice is intended to promote the greater good of all life, therefore much of it is about intentions. When practicing, you may discover that you need to proclaim that you wish to harm no one and that you will do everything in your power to protect all living beings on Earth.

This credo may be found in all Wiccan writings and has remained consistent and truthful for quite some time. It reminds you of your responsibility and power, and that you must make the right choice while using the gift of magic.

Equality

Coercion is not a part of the Wiccan religion. Proselytizing is discouraged, and an atmosphere of acceptance for different backgrounds and spiritual goals is promoted. Wiccans typically believe in equality in all areas and that everyone has the opportunity to choose their spiritual path, the one that is suitable for them.

The concept of equality should go without saying in all religions, yet this is not always the case. This is one of the ways that Wicca is unique; it offers a method to obtain wisdom and abundance through divine worship without implying that it must be done in a specific way.

Wicca means equality, and embracing this artistic religion necessitates an open heart and an open mind for anybody in search of a spiritual group and path.

The Rule of Three

Many Wiccan traditions employ the Threefold Law, often known as the Rule of Three. Although not everyone agrees with this commandment, it is frequently spoken and should be remembered or performed if it fits you. This notion holds that whatever spell or magical deed is performed, the generated energy will go into the Universe and return to the practitioner three times.

This concept may or may not be recognizable to you, and it has its roots in different cultural practices, particularly those of Eastern religions that believe in the law of karma. Wicca is responsible for the concept of three times, the number holding significance to the actuality of the power you wield.

It may not occur in the way you expect, for example, if you wish harm on someone else, you may have three different instances of ill fortune as a result, or the impact of the return may be little.

It is three times larger than it would ordinarily be, such as anticipating $100 and receiving $300. The Threefold Law is just another tool to help you maintain balance in your practice and ensure that you do not injure anyone, including yourself, with the energy of three returning to you.

All Things Have Elements

There are five elements in Wiccan belief: earth, air, fire, water, ether, or spirit. The five elements are summoned into balancing the energies of the ritual or spell throughout rituals and ceremonies, particularly while casting or consecrating a circle. Not all Wiccans practice with the five elements; some only use the four primary ones, preserving spirit as symbolized by the deity they serve.

These are the basic building components of everything on Earth and in the Universe. They are in charge of the immense endless cycle of life through creation and destruction, also known as the birth-death-rebirth cycle. These sacred natural elements are always present in Wiccan practice because they are the literal life force that connects all matter and all spirit.

These aspects have been researched throughout history and were part of ideologies dating back to the early Greeks, who also worshipped deities and practiced nature religions. These ideas can be found throughout continents in a variety of religions and philosophies, including Egypt and Babylonia, Hinduism and Buddhism, and many others.

The elements are unquestionably a necessary tool in Wiccan practice, and as you progress in your understanding of spell work and rituals, you will realize how significant and powerful they can be.

Beginning with the Fundamental Beliefs and Philosophies. This book serves as a starter kit for learning how to practice Wicca. It is a creative reality that necessitates comprehension of all of these fundamental, core aspects and concepts. Before you begin casting spells and crafting, you must first learn about the ideal manner to practice, as well as the principles and concepts that distinguish Wicca from other Pagan religions and rituals

The essential principles and philosophies presented in this chapter are only a starting point; you can learn more about these notions via your research and education in this profession. Consider this material to be a tool in your toolbox; it is the foundation of the house you will build with your starter kit to ensure that you are ready and equipped for the work ahead.

When you honor your decision to practice this amazing energetic truth, great things await you. It has limitless power and exists in everything, and the creative tools you use to connect to the work of Wicca will help you develop the practice that is suited for you on your journey.

Your Starter Kit's components are merely the beginning of a full expression of real Wiccan ceremony and practice. The presence and celebrations of the Sabbats and Esbats, as well as the rhythm and cycles they provide to the energy of your ongoing Wiccan rewards, will be covered in the following chapter.

Sun Cycles / Sabbats

Sabbats are the holidays, sometimes known as "solar holidays" or "time of the Sun," and are commemorated by the changing seasons via the Solstices and Equinoxes. Traditional holidays include the four solstices and equinoxes, as well as four additional holidays spread out throughout the year between these other big passes. The remaining four are usually located halfway between an equinox and a solstice.

You may notice in your rituals that some Wiccans refer to these times as the Higher and Lesser Sabbats, because the solstices and equinoxes are thought to be times of considerably greater intensity, and hence more worthy of celebration and importance.

It is only important in your practice that you devote some reflection and time to recognizing these moments in the

Earth's ever-changing cycles. You will discover that there are numerous methods to rejoice. You may find yourself creating your unique spells and rituals to practice these festivals with your Starter Kit.

Samhain (Lesser)

This is known as the New Year by witches. It's All Hallows Eve or Halloween, and the veil between the Earth and the spirit worlds is thin this time of year. This time of year signals the end of Summer and the beginning of the cold, winter months ahead when the Sun is less bright and the days are shorter. It is the cycle of the setting Sun and the arrival of darkness.

Many Wiccans regard this time as a time of personal death and rebirth when you delve within and contemplate what is to come in the following cycle. It is the time when you can preserve the fruits of your hard personal work and labor and be reminded of where you were and where you need to go before your magnificent rebirth in the Spring months.

Many individuals dress up as ghosts or spirits to honor the dead during this time. It is typically a time to honor deceased loved ones, and the ceremonies involved can be a gateway to communicating with the realm of spirits.

Yule (Greater)

Yule, also known as the Winter Solstice, has a pre-Christian name and origins in Pagan adoration of the divine in nature.

The Sun's position in the sky changes on this day. It is the longest night of the

The year before the days begin to lengthen again, bringing with them the hope of more light as Spring approaches.

It is a special time for bringing light into the home by candlelight, and many people will adorn their homes with pine and evergreen tree boughs and branches, as well as holly and mistletoe.

The Yule log is a wonderful custom on this day, and it is a sign of light to be lit all night long, recalling the energy of that life force in nature and welcoming it back into the changing seasons. This is also a suitable time to honor the Goddesses because it is their season when the Sun's light is fading and the nights are longer. This is an excellent time for reflection, and it prepares you for the brighter days ahead.

Imbolc (Lesser)

This sacred event, a season of regeneration, purity, fertility, and growth, is under the hands of the Goddess Brigid, a maiden form of the Triple Goddess. It occurs at the beginning of February and heralds the arrival of spring and the awakening of the maiden. The last frosts are falling, and the white of snow and ice is melting.

It is a moment to let go of the old and prepare for the new, which is just around the corner. A period of regeneration is approaching.

Ostara (Greater) is the Spring Equinox and represents the ideal balance of light and dark. The marriage, or union, of the god and the goddess, or the sun and the moon, is thought to bring light back into the world and announce fresh growth. This time of year is represented by the goddess Ostara. Her name is derived from the Greek word desire, which means "egg," as in a new egg of spring, ready to hatch and give birth to new life.

It is a time to rejoice in the regeneration of the male and female energies of Earth and spirit, as well as your internal balances.

Beltane (Lesser) Many people refer to this occasion as May Day since it usually falls on the first of May and represents the halfway point between the Spring equinox and the summer solstice. It is a cry to the fertility and abundance of gods as people celebrate the consummation of the god and goddess' marriage to sow new life in the soils of the Earth's womb.

The Maypole is a symbol of this time and is danced around to commemorate the occasion, and bonfires are an important component of the festivities, drawing attention to the growing power of the sun's masculine force as it develops in strength and length of time in the sky. With the waxing sunshine and the great goddess of fertility, preparing to give birth to the burgeoning seed within her womb, it is a period of bounty, abundance, and fertility.

Lithe (Greater)

Lithe is another name for the Summer Solstice, which occurs in June. It represents the point in the Earth's cycle when the sun is at its strongest before it begins to wane in preparation for Autumn. This holiday, also known as Mid-Summer Night's Eve, is the time when the fairies appear and partake in the fun and celebration. Because of the nearby fairies' enchantment, it has been seen as an excellent period for divination.

Another opportunity to appreciate the Sun's vitality and the burning passion that resides in the hotter, brighter months of the year. This is a time to conserve energy and prepare for the upcoming harvest, which will carry you into Autumn.

Lughnasadh (Lesser)

Lughnasadh, also known as Lammas, marks the beginning of the harvest and the conclusion of the Sun's greatest period. The fertility goddess is giving birth to all that developed in the soil of her womb throughout the light months. It is now time to set away and store the bounty of this big birthing in preparation for the colder months ahead. It is the period between when the Earth turns chilly and rests and when the underworld opens. This is a time to be appreciative and grateful, admiring Mother Earth's bounty and reflecting on the offering of the Sun's energy and light in all of the plants and foods collected. Mabon (Greater) Mabon marks the Autumnal Equinox and is the second harvest, following

Samhain. This is the time of year when the leaves begin to change color and welcome a new type of late to the day, heralding the end of fertility and abundance. It is a time of storage, preparation, protection, security, and grounding, and it awakens the new hours of daylight and night before the witch's new year to restart the cycle. This is a tremendous moment to give appreciation to the spirit world's aging god and goddess as they enter their crone years and the Great Mother rests from her time of giving birth to the cycles and celebrations of all life. We embrace the age of night and the cold season so that the mother crone can rest and regenerate before bringing life back into the earth in the spring.

Moon Cycles / Esbats

Every four weeks, the moon becomes pregnant with Goddess light, which illuminates the night sky. These monthly moon cycles function in combination with the Sabbats to mark the Sun's trip, and the goddess moon is the polar opposite of the Sun's light, bringing aquatic balance to the heat. During the esbats, the moon and the force of the triple goddess (Maiden-Mother-Crone) are celebrated, as is her holy light. Some people operate in groups or covens, such as with Sabbat celebrations and festivals, but any solitary practitioner can celebrate Sabbat or Esbat on their own, and partake in the knowing and awareness that many Wiccans throughout the world are staring at the same orb of light as you are. It is a powerful spell to perform everything at once, which is why it is critical to creating time for this moment.

Esbats and the Triple Goddess

The sort of activity, such as a Sabbat celebration, ritual, or spell, differs from individual to person or coven to coven. One constant is the worship of the triple goddess in connection with the moon rites. The Triple Goddess is the only one who appears all year. She is Maiden in the Spring, merging in union with the Sun God before becoming Mother in the Summer months, nurturing and gestating the rich fruits of Earth. Finally, she is elevated to Crone in the Autumn/Winter months, when her energies are those of a wise old lady preparing for her rebirth into maidenhood. You may decide to revere a specific form of the Triple Goddess during the Sabbat cycles. For example, in Spring ritual esbats, you may find ways to honor the Maiden goddesses, such as Brigid or Ostara, under the full moonlight, or the crone goddesses, such as Hecate, under the Autumn and Winter moons.

Rituals for the Full Moon

It is standard tradition to hold a ceremony, or ritual, or cast a spell while the full moon shines down on you. Wiccans who operate in covens will have their own, specialized tasks to undertake, while solitary practitioners will use their energies to identify the needs of the moon they are dealing with. you could be casting magic for personal reasons, or you could be harnessing the moon's power to bring peace and prosperity to all people. A ritual or incantation is a frequent practice during an esbat, regardless of how you choose to interact with the full moon. However, some esbats may be little more than a practice of thankfulness and thanksgiving; a moment of reverence for the immense divine. It only matters if you have a lot of practice. It is also not necessary to designate a specific deity or goddess. Many Wiccans will simply mention the Triple Goddess' name and use her entire energy as a symbol of all the power and energy of the moon and the cycles of life.

Rituals for the New Moon

Let us not overlook the New Moon. Wiccans do not always worship the full moon, and it is customary to choose another cycle, in this case, the new moon. Some regard it as the ideal time to honor the goddess, and you may discover that many covens or solitary practitioners prefer to work with the energy of the dark moon, drawing attention to a ritual or spell and allowing it to blossom with the waxing moon. It depends on what sort of which you are or want to be, therefore when it comes to esbat practices and rituals, you have the power of choice. Another widespread practice is to have esbats for four moons every month, commemorating not only the full and new moons but also the first and last quarter moons. A wonderful method to respect the goddess and the cycles of the year is to ask for all wisdom from the waxing and waning of the moon. The esbats are a strong source of connection to the divine rhythms of life in your Wicca practice when used in conjunction with the sabbats, or solar cycles.

Wicca 101

This brief overview of Wicca is merely a beginning point, an egg of Spring, to get you started with your practice. Knowledge of what you are about to align with is a crucial aspect of any magical starter kit, and it is critical that you understand the traditions, concepts, and beliefs before you begin your practice. There may be a lot more knowledge out there in the world, and you should keep looking and asking questions. Wicca is a huge and diverse world that speaks to a wide range of methods, deities, rituals, and spells. You'll want to learn more as you go, and our Starter Kit is a terrific way to get you pumped up with magical life force so you can begin practicing right away. When you are ready to begin practicing, you can refer to my other book, Wicca for

Beginners: A Basic Guide for the Modern Age to Learn About the Mysteries of Wiccan Beliefs and History, and How to Use Candles, Crystals, Herbs, Magic Rituals, and Spells, to help guide you through even more details of Wiccan worship, spells, and rituals, and to keep you on track with your study of this magical craft.

Chapter 2

What Do You Need‚?

Wicca's Basic Tools

Wicca is a creative practice with no doctrines; instead, there are guidelines, beliefs, and philosophies that encourage you to perform magic responsibly. It is totally up to you which tools you use, and you may take great joy in designing some of your own. It is a fascinating trip to construct your magic using your own, created tools, and if you feel more confident in your knowledge and practice, you will value that aspect of your magic skills. Meanwhile, to get you started, this chapter shows a list of some of the more regularly used tools for rituals and spells. You may not need or want all of these goods to begin, but they provide a strong foundation for comprehending some of what you may encounter on your journey.

Purchasing Equipment for the Starter Kit

There are numerous ways to create your toolbox, and you don't have to spend a lot of money to get what you need. There are always cheaper alternatives to the more expensive products you can find in a New-Age shop or online, but if you're curious, go ahead and do it. There is something to be said for holding something in your hand before purchasing it, and while online shopping is convenient, it may not always be the greatest option when procuring your sacred tools, unless it is from a reputable source. The fun of Wicca is how creative it is, and how you may spend time seeking for stuff from what you currently own and may have that will provide you with just what you need. You may have some old kitchen items that are utterly non-magical, but once blessed and consecrated to perform magic, they will appear entirely different to you and will make fantastic altar equipment moving forward. If you're crafty and want to get truly creative, you can also manufacture a lot of your tools, or you can slowly collect things from local businesses and nature. The most magical approach to obtaining the tools you truly desire is to send out your intention to the universe and ask for the appropriate ones to come to you. Keep a watch out for them as they will appear gradually and possibly when you least expect it. They could be a gift at times, or you could trip over them in a parking lot outside the grocery store. With magic, you never know, so keep a watch out for any equipment you're seeking to attract to yourself.

Cleaning Your Equipment

Before you utilize any item, you obtain, it is critical that you cleanse and consecrate it to clear it of any previous energy and make it your own for magical purposes. Because everything is energy and everything carries energy, even if something indicates it has already been cleansed or sanctified, cleanse it regardless.

Your magical instruments must carry the pure essence of you and you're practice, and a simple cleansing ceremony can be performed with your number one tool, the elements, and the casting of a circle. It's all about intentions, so smudge the energy with incense while incanting some words about your intentions with the tools, offering that any previous ownership and reality be relinquished. It doesn't have to be difficult, just deliberate.

Gather Your Tools Using Your Intuition

It always depends on the ritual and what you want to achieve, but a good rule of thumb is to have a tool for each element in the circle, i.e., earth, air, fire, and water. You'll see which represents which in later parts, but for now, you can get the concept that your ritual tools are here to help boost the energy of the spell work you're conducting.

The most crucial thing is that you are pulled to and have an energetic connection to whatever tool you are utilizing.

If a particular tool does not feel right for the ritual you are performing,

Correct, do not use it. It might not be the best energy for your spell, and that's fine. Wicca practice is learning to trust one's instincts and honoring what feels right for each new magical encounter.

Tools are not a required component in Wicca magic, and you may have felt that you don't need any tools and that all you need is yourself and nature, which is completely fine. You can use your power and energy to draw into the divine life forces, but this takes time and effort, so having your altar of instruments is a fantastic method to honor and direct the energies you need to keep and work with while you're getting started.

Let's take a look at some of the tools you might wish to incorporate into your practice and how they can affect your spells and rituals.

The Components

Why are the elements seen as a tool in Wicca? The four basic elements, together with a fifth of spirit, are one of the most important instruments in your practice. You will almost always honor and call the elements into your circle when executing a ceremony. If anything, the elements are the most important tool in your toolbox and should be treated as such. Consider them a tool for connecting with the divine and making intentions for protection and manifestation. These aspects are always present in any magic you practice and serve to widen your degrees of magical force by incorporating them into your spells. Typically, the elements are invoked at the beginning of a ceremony, with each element connected with a cardinal direction — North, East, South, West, or Earth, Air, Fire, Water. When using these instruments, you should usually acknowledge them by facing each direction that they represent. If you are unsure of which direction to take, you should carry a compass with you. This procedure is also known as "calling the quarters," which is just the act of calling the elements and directions. Typically, the same action is carried out.

when the ritual or circle is closed in the same way that it was opened furthermore, each element can be represented by several of the tools discussed in this chapter. For example, the pentacle symbol represents the Earth element and the North and can be used in rituals ranging from earthly anchoring to giving focus to earth energies. Another example is a candle flame, which represents the element of fire, and so forth. The same may be said for each crystal or plant you utilize in your practice. They all have unique features and properties to investigate, and will always have a connection to one of the elements, if not more, based on your intuition about what you're dealing with. Objects have the same effect. River stones indicate water, but depending on your practice, they could also represent soil. Feathers can signify air, for example.

The Elements are your primary tool, so become acquainted with them and what they may symbolize in your toolbox.

The Boiling Pot

Throughout history and popular culture, this tool has been associated with witchcraft. It is a symbol of magic and has been depicted as an important tool in the witch's job. It is a magical cooking pot, and it is related to both fire and water. The water, potion, or brew is held in the cauldron, but it cannot boil or appear without the heat and flame of the fire burning beneath its belly.

It represents the creative force of transformation as portrayed by the Goddess in Wiccan beliefs. The Goddess exists in all of her incarnations throughout the year, just as the cauldron fires the same transformation in everything it bears within it.

In modern times, the cauldron is not essential to your practice, but it is an excellent tool for magical work, particularly with fire, or as a safe location to burn candles and other magical ingredients such as herbs and incense. You might even want to utilize it to make a potion, but you'll need to be able to create a blazing fire below it, which isn't easy or desirable for indoor magical work cauldron can also be used for scrying and divination. A drop of sacred water in the cauldron to gaze at will unlock certain doors to the divine's secrets. It may be your incense burner and magical herb burner on the altar. Cauldrons can be purchased at stores as well as online magic stores. They are not as common as candles or incense, but they are an excellent addition to your beginner set. They are available in several sizes that you can select based on your need. A smaller cauldron is ideal for a lone practitioner or any type of indoor practice. altar or workstation They are available in a variety of metals, with cast iron being the most common, and they stand on three legs with a handle. It must be transported safely. It's okay if you can't find a cauldron! You can use another type of heat-safe bowl that is just as magical until you find the cauldron you have summoned.

The Athame's

The athame is a blade or a sword that is used for direct and cutting energy, representing transformation and is considered the element of fire (or air, depending on whichever Wiccan magic you are practicing). It possesses powerful, masculine energy and is hence associated with God's energy rather than goddess energy. Swords are forged in fire, and the metal of the blade is directed into becoming a sturdy blade of intention and purpose once melted and liquid. It resembles a dagger and often has a black handle, or hilt, and is no longer than the length of your hand. They are available in stores or as gifts and are far more difficult to construct on your own than some of the other instruments. Athames with crystal or stone blades can sometimes be found in online or local shops. If you can't afford a fine athame, you can consecrate a little kitchen knife and include it into your magical toolbox, endowing it with the authority and power of your Wiccan practice.

In general, cutting anything with an athame is solely symbolic in the ritual sense; but modern Wiccans will use their athame to cut herbs in the wild, carve wands and remove the branch or twig from the tree, and carve pentacles and other magical symbols into various spells and ritual materials. Wicca will always desire a fire element, and a dagger, or athame, is the perfect combination of the sun's fiery and masculine energy, as well as its direct drive to cut through energy and bring about a tremendous fullness to your rituals. Keep an athame as a tool and cleanse it frequently with your other magical instruments.

The Trophy

The term chalice refers to a cup or goblet. It is associated with the element of water and the Goddess's spirit. It represents abundance and fertility and can play a variety of functions in the rituals and spells you choose to cast. It is frequently regarded as an offering, or a means of presenting presents or libations to the deities summoned to your ritual.

It can hold whatever liquid seems appropriate for your ritual: water, wine, ale, tea, kombucha, essences, and potions. In contrast, an empty chalice can be symbolic in certain rites, suggesting a receptivity to receive abundance from the spiritual world.

The chalice in most traditional Wiccan practice is silver in color and made of metal as a depiction of the Goddess and the moon.

You might not want to drink from a silver-plated or pewter cup, so even if you locate one like this at a Magic Shoppe, you probably won't be able to drink from it regularly due to poisonous compounds and elements. Certain beverages can corrode these metals, rendering them unsafe for consumption.

It is not required while constructing your tool kit, and you can bless and consecrate any cup that feels like the proper choice for your altar and your way of honoring the vast divine. You may already be aware of one that is ideal for your purposes, and all you need to do is cast magical intentions around it. A wine glass can be as powerful as a goblet purchased from a neo-pagan shop. There could also be a cup that has been passed down through your family.

For a long time, honoring your ancestors with your magical chalice seemed like a wonderful choice. You can also keep an eye out for anything that catches your eye while shopping around town. It is usually better to avoid using plastic or synthetic materials in any instruments you acquire for magical reasons. Treat your chosen cup differently than your other cups. It should not be washed in the dishwasher because it is used for magical reasons and should be considered sacred to you and you're practice.

Smoke and incense

Incense has been used in many religious civilizations since antiquity. It has always permeated the halls and realms of focused purposeful practices of connection to spirit, and it is an important aspect of many cultural rites today. It is an aromatic tool that combines earthly components such as herbs, spices, tree bark, oils, and resins to produce smoke of cleaning purity, producing sacred space and air in the atmosphere. It is related to the element of Air (and occasionally fire) and is a common component of Wiccan rituals and spells.

Traditional incense burning methods include the use of loose herbs in a censer. A censer is a suspended container that can be swung from a rope, chain, or handle. Catholic priests frequently use a censer in their liturgies. You can also use your tiny cauldron as a censer, wafting the smoke around and allowing it to burn in your cauldron as you execute your rituals.

Working with loose incense might be difficult. You will normally need some charcoal bricks or discs, which are sold with incense in many stores. Sticks or cones are a more popular type of incense these days, and depending on your setup and tools and procedures, they can be easier and perhaps safer to burn. Either way will work perfectly well. Smudge sticks, which are often merely a bundle of wrapped, dry herbs that you can light and then let smoke, are also available. Smudging is another common way to consecrate your holy place by working with air energy. Palo Santo is a sacred, harvested wood that comes in little sticks and can be ignited and burned for the same purposes.

Incense is frequently considered an offering to whatever deities you are connecting with, and you can burn it to a picture of them on your altar or establish the intention that you are concentrating on that specific god or goddess as it burns. Using incense during rituals and spells is quite potent, and you can change the aroma depending on the spell. The earthly things used to manufacture incense, like herbs and spices, all convey different energies, so be sure you're dealing with the correct fragrant energy for your spell work.

Smoke is purifying and cleaning, and it is excellent for dispelling negative energies. It is capable of preparing for Wiccan practice as well as casting a circle. It is a potent instrument that you should employ frequently in all of your magical activities.

The Lighter

The candle represents all of the elements. The wick represents the Earth and must be present to root the candle and keep it lit and burning. The wax is water in the sense that it melts, transforms into liquid, and then evaporates, exhibiting water's transformational properties. Air is essential to keep the candle flame burning because there would be no fire without oxygen. The flare is unmistakable:

fire. When you charge the candle to infuse spirit into the candle's elements, you add the fifth element. All five elements combined in one candle equals a potent magical tool, unifying all of the forces of the universe in one small item.

Candles enable us to incorporate the magical power of color into our spells and crafts. Certain colors are connected with different aspects of life and can be used to represent magical training Correlating colors to related spells results in a more potent intention and manifestation.

You can amp up the potency of your candle tool by anointing it with sacred or magical oils and smells to spread your message even further. Working with specific herbs and consecrated oils will always give the energy of your candle magic more power, and so the candle is a very powerful little tool that should be incorporated into almost every ritual, with the combination of all of the elements, the possibilities of color magic, and the enhancement of power through oils and herbs.

The Stone and the Crystal

Crystal is a broad phrase that can refer to a variety of solid things used in Wiccan rituals. Simply put, crystals are minerals.

Minerals are inorganic substances that originate and grow naturally underground on the Earth's surface. Why they are classified as "inorganic" by science is beyond the comprehension of a Wiccan, who regards minerals and crystals as living beings. Because each crystal, stone, and mineral has its distinct energy and chemical composition, they reflect extremely varied energies and attributes.

Most minerals' unique forms and patterns are caused by their molecular structure, which also provides some flat surfaces and intriguing geometric formations. Quartz crystal, rose quartz, amethyst, and other crystals are commonly utilized in magical practices. These are crystalline, as opposed to some of the other precious stones that are as valued in the usage of magic. These stones include jade, kyanite, lapis lazuli, tiger's eye, and others. Unlike their crystalline counterparts, these stones are made up of various minerals and hence are not what we call "real crystals," yet they still have a lot of energy and force. Crystals and stones, whatever you call them, are Earth's gifts that hold immense magic. They are commonly employed in magical circles and Wiccan ceremonies. They can be utilized to heal one's energy as well as the energy of plants and animals. You may even Crystals and stones are charged with electricity and are sensitive to the elements. They are energy conduits that can help you bring in and send out energy through your ritual activities. Keeping a collection of crystals and stones for use in your Wicca practice is a simple method to increase the manifestation and potency of your daily rituals and spells.

When performing your opening ceremonies, you might utilize them to mark your sacred circle. They can be used to commemorate specific deities associated with particular stones. When employed in personal energy cleaning, they can change and shift your energy from a low to a high frequency. They can be worn as protective jewelry. They can be incorporated into charms, amulets, and sachets. You can use them for scrying and divination, or just to focus your ritual. Consider using color magic with gemstones and stones. They come in a variety of mystical colors, and depending on your job, the extra benefit of specific stones and the colors that they bring can further strengthen your manifestation methods.

The Plants

When it comes to Wicca, herbs are unquestionably tools. Herbal magic has a long history and is one of the key components of any type of healing herbal medicine or magic spell utilized in many forms of Paganism.

Herbs have a special history with witches and have been around longer than any other drug or remedy, and they will continue to outlive and outlast the drugstore meds that are so popular now.

Aside from their healing effects, which each lonely Wiccan should investigate, they all have very powerful magical properties. A variety of herbs cultivated in your backyard garden will always come in handy for your rituals and creative projects.

People will use herbs to decorate their Sabbat and Esbat altars, as well as to carry around on their person for protection or other magical purposes. The use of herbs as a tool in Wicca is something to become familiar with. They are adaptable and will serve several functions with all of the spells you cast. If you regularly practice Wicca, keeping a cabinet of dried herbs is a good idea, and you should consider them just as significant as any other gear on the list. You can burn them as incense, make a charm or sachet, or even use them in a spell for a healing remedy ritual, taking your herbs in the form of tea, tincture, or broth. All of your herbs, like all of your other instruments, can be charged and consecrated before use. As you practice more Wicca rituals and spells, you will discover new and inventive uses for the great range of herbs available, as well as what all of their magical purposes are.

The Pentacle.

Although not every pentacle is a five-pointed star, that is the most typically inscribed symbol known as the pentacle. A pentacle is just a disk-shaped slab with one or more magical symbols etched on it. The five-pointed star is the most prevalent in Wicca, therefore for the sake of this book, you can assume that when I speak to a pentacle, I am referring to that shape. Because the five-pointed star is also known as a pentagram, it is a simple word to identify with the common pentacle. The pentagram is an old sign and symbol seen all over the world in numerous cultures to represent a multitude of characteristics of the human mind, body, and spirit. It is an Earth symbol, and the pentacle pentagram represents the terrestrial emblems on the cards in the sacred Tarot deck. The star's points reflect the elements, with the top point representing spirit. The rounded shape and earthy feel firmly identify it with the Goddess. Wiccans will inscribe a pentacle on the hilt of their athame or the cover of their Book of Shadows. It can also be used to sanctify an area or ritual by drawing a symbol in the air with a wand or blade, or even with a smoky incense or smudge stick. It is a powerful manifestation tool as well as a helpful symbol of protection against dangerous or perhaps negative energy. If you have a huge pentacle, you can utilize it as a consecration tool by placing additional magical tools or components, like candles or crystals, on top of it to fill it with sacred, symbolic energy. For ritual and spell work, you can even carve a pentacle into the wax of a candle, or simply sketch it on objects with a marker or ink. Pentacles can be found in the majority of magical shops and online retailers. They are available in a range of shapes, sizes, and materials. Many Wiccans will wear a pentacle as a protective talisman or amulet, as well as a symbol of their trade. You can be a creative individual who wants to construct your pentacle at home using your materials. There is no right or wrong way to do it as long as you use your manifestation of magic to construct it for ceremonial purposes. If you only have paper and a pen, you can sculpt it out of clay, carve it into the wood, or paint it on a canvas; the possibilities are unlimited. The pentacle is a potent elemental sign of protection and manifestation that you can add to your beginning kit. Use it wisely and liberally.

The Magic Wand

The wand is a prominent emblem of witchcraft that stretches back to Egypt's forebears as well as ancient Pagan societies.

Wands are the manifestation and directing instruments that relate to the element of Air. The air element is also represented by the suit of wands in the Tarot and deals with the power of thinking and intentions.

Despite the popularity of certain fictional magical witches and wizards, In today's entertainment world, television is not the wand itself that contains the magic; the witch is the one who imbues the wand with power to develop and manifests their power and life force energy by use of ritual intention It is utilized to assist the direst unsubtly way. and soft manner (as opposed to the athame, which is a bit more intense in its manner).

A wand is frequently used in rituals to invoke the deities you worship are inviting people into your magical circle and can also be used for Magical symbols, such as the pentagram, drawn in the air. Symbols of the pentacle This tool represents the gods more than anything else than goddesses, as evidenced by its phallic form (also like the athame) but also because of the way it focuses energy in a more masculine manner force. The wand, depending on the type of Wicca you practice, In general, is connected with air, although it can also be related to fire. because of its transforming and mystical abilities Regarding As a solo Wiccan, you can do whatever seems right for you.

There may be a more deliberate or particular choice in some covens, according to that group Finding the correct wand for you can be an interesting journey. They can be obtained in a variety of methods. Many Wiccans will discover their wands from the local magic shop, which has a broad variety of designs, including those made of crystals and gemstones stones that have a lot of tremendous energy other wands can be built by hand and for a creative touch,

This is the finest option. Whatever wand you create with your own hands Your energy and power will generate even more powerful magic for you. Nature can provide you with the tools for your homemade wand. You will need to rely on your intuition to direct you to the appropriate materials. You might discover the right tree branch to transform into a wand, but you must always get permission from the tree first. Watch for the Respond and explain your goals with it. It could be exciting to transform into your wand!

There are numerous additional natural gifts from the land that might be enjoyed. Twigs, moss, feathers, and other natural materials can be used to make wands. leaves, whatever seems appropriate for you Whether you make a wand or not or you purchase one, it is a highly useful tool for giving you greater directness in your spells and rituals, as well as assisting you in attracting more masculine energy and incorporating an air element into your work

Shadows in the Book

This is frequently one of the most prized instruments in a witch's armory.

Your Book of Shadows is your unique spell book. A book that will help you through whatever you do It is the location of all of your rituals, spells, symbols, prayers, poems, recipes, and sacred texts

Information is saved. It is an excellent location for you to keep track of your Wicca will also develop and evolve as you travel through it like tremendous living energy, you'reractise

A coven's handbook is what they follow as a group, and much knowledge, such as family traditions and customs, is passed down through generations' stories. It is the finest way for you to progress as a single practitioner your spells and practice, one page at a time over the years

The Book of Shadows has a lengthy history, and it was Gerald who created it. Gardner is credited with coining the term "Wiccan practice." A Collection of Shadows cast by others are frequently added to generationally and Some Wiccans have even created their version of the Book of the Dead.

assist Wiccans on their way who require a safe place to stay start. You can create your Book by using the spells and rituals of others. People who have gone before you, and continue to contribute to it as you grow and evolve tweaking and modifying numerous spells to improve your craft and meet your requirements It is an excellent method for you to organize the greatest and most beneficial spells you come across on your journey You may have several options numerous craft books, but you only use a selection of them diverse rituals from your library of witchcraft. A Book of shadows is a fantastic technique for you to get the correct information for your solitary practice and make your spells out of it.

It is effectively your Physician's Desk Reference for magic, and the more you add to it and use it, the better you will get at

boosting your magical practice. You can design it however you

like and locate a certain notebook that speaks deeply with you

and your energy. In these modern times, you can also keep your

book of shadows in digital form, on your home computer, or even

online on a website, to show others who are interested in your work. This can be good, however, ourysphysicalrmats, like ink and pap have a more visceral impact on the work of spells and magic. You may want to consider transcribing your Book

of Shadows digitally for safekeeping but have an original copy that is a physical book.

This tool will be with you the whole way. It is your guidebook and travel map through your rituals, spells, and incantations and it will always be a grounding and supportive energy in your toolbox.

The Tarot is a deck of 78 cards that each represent important archetypes and symbols. The origins of the Tarot are separate from Wiccan and other Pagan practices that have been around as early as the 1400s. People who are not at all interested in Wicca or magic find themselves drawn to this humble deck of cards. They are a way to answer questions through imagery and symbols and have been used in various forms of divination, prediction, and manifestation. The messages of the cards and the spread that they are in allow us to ask for direct consultation with the divine life forces to gain knowledge and understanding of what is happening in our lives. It is a reflection of life, or a cosmic mirror, that allows the questioner to get a deeper truth to their queries. You can see beyond what you would normally choose to see and there are new angles to consider and support your path ahead.

The art of reading the Tarot cards is a whole other kind of magic that takes time and practice and when you bond with the cards, they bond with you, too. Many witches are very careful about how they come by their decks, or "choose" them. Some say they should only be given as a gift, and others note that it is best to be guided to the right deck to support your power and magical purposes and

intentions.

The standard deck is 78 cards, divided into a Major and Minor Arcana. Each section, and each card within that section, reflect inner truths and deeper, hidden knowledge. The whole deck is a long story of a traveler going through a journey and that journey is depicted in various images that support the natural powers of the Earth, including all five elements, as well as sun and moon energy, masculine and feminine polarities, and astrology.

The Major Arcana are the most powerful cards in the deck and are indications that you will be experiencing powerful shifts and upheavals, whether good or bad, in your life. The characters on the cards, or archetypes, represent an important stage in the questioner's journey ranging from the pure innocence of the Fool to the hard-earned wisdom of the World. There are deep and

meaningful lessons shown in the Major Arcana and it is a good choice to pay attention when these cards show up as an influence. The rest of the deck is the Minor Arcana and is very similar to a deck of regular playing cards. Each number, from Ace to 10, has each element associated with it on a different card. There are 4 aces in the deck, one for Earth, Air, Fire, and Water. Therefore, it is for the Two, the three, and so on. They are depicted on the cards, instead of as the elements, as the Pentacles, Wands, Swords, and Cups. Look familiar? All of the suits are represented by the tools you are learning about to represent your magical work with your practice.

These cards are thought to be more about the everyday ions we take in life, rather than the profound spiritual journey of the Major Arcana. They cover the elements of the experience, not

the experience itself. Those elements fall into the categories of manifestation and roundedness (pentacles), ideas and thoughts (wands), action and direction (swords), and feelings and emotions

(cups).

As you can see, there is overlap and connection between the Tarot and Wicca, as well as other forms of witchcraft. The cards are even linked to other occult philosophies including numerology and astrology. Each card can be linked to a celestial body or zodiac sign, as well as a number, based on the card's suit and where it falls in the order for the deck.

Tarots can be incorporated as symbolic representations of certain elements or factors in your spell work and rituals.

You can use each card for specific reasons, like a Full Moon ritual incorporating The

Moon card on your altar or in your spells, or the use of the Sun card in a prosperity or abundance spell. You can even use the deck as a consult to help you design your spells and rituals.

Tarot cards are universally used for a variety of reasons and have very close ties to the practice of Wicca. They are an incredible tool to help with divination and consulting the divine to help you manifest the appropriate stage of your trip through rituals and spells

Your Toolbox & Beginning Kit

Each of the tools provided in this chapter is an excellent place to begin every Wiccan Each one may come to you as a separate impact at different times. at various periods as you add to your toolbox, or you may discover They can begin cleaning and disinfecting them all at once. sacrificing them for your magical purposes Make it clear what you want your tools to be. Create your altar and your creative abundance and vitality into your toolkit If this is the case,

If you're interested in joining a coven, your organization may put you in the right direction. obtain certain tools You can govern the solitary practitioner your options more freely and take your time in finding Whichever tools feel appropriate for you Use your instincts to get what you want. Allow the tools to find you and be prepared for them when they arrive.

The following step will teach you explains how to make an
altar with all of your magical tools to get you going

Chapter 3

Altars: A Step-by-Step Guide

What exactly is an altar? Altars have existed across cultures and religions and throughout time, and continue to represent a physical expression of our devotion to the divine It is the location where we

are on a beautiful day to celebrate our gods, goddesses, ancestors, and spirits Any ritual, celebration, magic, meditation, or prayer must have a focal point. The altar you create is the focal point of your Wiccan practice. and it constantly makes room for all of the holy aspects that you introduce into your life Wiccan altars can be created indoors, outdoors, or both. Because you aren't

They are frequently found in settings where they can perform rituals all day. They can be off to the side but seen frequently, or they can be hauled out to be noticed and displayed in the room's middle for spell work and rituals Typically, all of the tools you use for your craftwork and spells are included. stay on the altar at all times and are typically visible as part of the sacrifice. If you have an outdoor altar, you can utilize an entirely different design. You'll need a different set of tools for your outdoor altar than you would for your interior altar.

As you learned in the last chapter, the tools you employ are symbols for the divine parts of nature recognized and asserted by Wicca as part of the enchantment of being connected to the rhythms and cycles of all life This contains the tools of the five elements as well as the gods. Goddesses who have been chosen for worship Some altars are reflections of the admiration for these deities through the display of images or statues or figurines honoring that particular deity, as well as the elements

Candles, chalice, athame, wand, and other items are used to symbolize this. Many altars attempt to embrace the elements by incorporating a dish of a bowl of salt and water (salt can be replaced with dirt or sand to symbolize ground energy). The candle serves as both a fire and an altar.

To indicate air, an incense holder or burner is generally present. Another tool that was not mentioned in the previous chapter but is frequently utilized in. A bell is used in ritual practice and to embellish an altar.

A bell is an excellent method to draw attention to your altar and allow that sound to be heard. You are worshipping the altar of magic with wave energy. Bell the tone is also very open and helps you focus your energies convconvertingrgy all around into devotion An altar bell is an excellent source of directing energy to what the altar signifies to you

Step-by-Step Instructions for Building an Altar

Here's where you should start when constructing your altar. Take it one step at a time, and keep in mind that your altar will change as you practice.

So, it doesn't have to be perfect from the start.

Step 1: Select the Best Location

Your altar could assume any number of forms and be housed in any number of locations in a range of settings Your home may have a built-in shelf or cupboard.

You may need to use a home that is the perfect size and location, or you may need to utilize a piece of furniture that serves as a flat platform on which to set

Set up your altar.

You might not be able to afford to buy a new piece of furniture right away furniture to serve as your altar and thus a temporary solution, such as a desk Alternatively, a coffee table will suffice. You can put it wherever. Place it wherever it won't get in the way of your rituals and draw it out as needed.

and spell check Many people will use a square or rectangular surface, but many will utilize a round or oval surface. Wiccans prefer round table tops because they are easier to maneuver around.

and is associated with the moon, the sun, and the deity as well as other symbols used in the craft

Altars are typically composed of natural materials, and it is best to try and

Choose wood furniture or locations for your altar.

Metal is occasionally used. Glass surfaces are also popular. In general, it is

It is typical to use a cloth or tapestry to cover the

It is on the table's surface. This cloth can be magically charged.

using a ritual

Wherever you choose to place your altar, it must contain the elements listed below:

Accessible

Made from natural materials (if possible)

Movable (if possible or desired)

Always visible to you (if preferred- you may also select to).

To avoid contamination, keep it hidden in a cupboard or covered with a cloth.

preventing visitors from meddling with it)

Once you've determined the location and surface for your altar,

be in, you can start setting it up and preparing it for ritual magic.

work of magic

Step 2: Prepare your Altar

1. Use your chosen cloth to cover the surface. It could have been

infused with defensive energy, or you could have a significant

heirloom garment, such as a scarf, from a deceased relative or ancestor

Whatever cloth you choose, is intended to set the tone for your altar.

space, and it may become soiled with candle wax, ashes, or other debris

plants, incense, and magical equipment, so be certain it's a cloth you're using.

don't mind being smudged by magical use

2. Choose and display a focal piece for your altar. The

Its focal point could be a specific depiction of a god or goddess.

goddesses, pentacles, candles, big geodes, crystals, or stones

It is up to you to select how you wish to focus your attention.

altar and direct your attention to the focal point of your magical

practice. It's a good idea to start from the center focus point because

You can use your other tools to work around it.

3. Include your tools, whatever they are. You might want to

Determine the orientation of your altar at this time. This

could also have an impact on where you set your altar.

You may prefer that it face a specific direction, in which case you will

That must be accommodated first before the rest of it can be put up.

When arranging your precious tools, you may want to

Sort them according to their cardinal directions. For example:

Position the athame (fire) to the south.

Place the chalice (water) to the west.

Place the incense (air) to the east.

Place the pentacle (Earth) to the north.

Placing your tools in the directions they represent can help you stay focused on the elements and how they perform in your rituals. Fill the chalice with water, add a bowl of soil or salt, then replace the pentacle with a feather for the eastern air and candles for the south. What artifacts you choose to place are entirely up to you, but they should all be a regular component of your magical rituals.

4. Another alternative is to position your Goddess tools on the left (Earth and Water) and the God tools on the right (Fire and Air). It all depends on the type of Wicca you want to practice on your altar.

5. Eclectic practitioners (typically solitary) may design and create their altar based on their thoughts and preferences; therefore, it can follow any natural structure and arrangement based on your practice.

6. Consecrate your altar by lighting a candle and burning incense and asking the elements to bless your location. At this stage, you can cast a circle or execute a ritual (see Chapters 4 and 5), or you can keep it simple by bringing focus and intention to celebrating the creation of your altar with a few simple tools and words. Allow your candle to burn until

it burns out, and maintain some incense burning to bring the altar to life.

7. Maintain a clean, well-organized, and revered altar. As you use your altar more frequently, you may need to cleanse and purify it regularly. Maintain the altar's freshness and fluidity so that your magic does not become stagnant.

8. Decorate your altar by the holiday you are commemorating. At Yule or Samhain, your entire home may become an altar, but your actual shrine requires some additional special items to help you honor the Wheel Honoré Year and maintain this throughout tidiness seasons.

Clearing and Charging Your Altar and Tools

Over time, your equipment and altar might accumulate undesirable or negative energy. Even brand-new instruments purchased via the internet may include unwanted energy that must be removed from the manufacturing, packaging, and shipping procedures. During spells and rituals, or even when you have a large number of guests in your home surrounding your altar, your environment and the objects you use can collect and absorb energy that has to be cleared.

It is a good habit to develop and is simple to implement.

You may require a different purifying agent depending on the object you are attempting to clean. Let's have a look at a few of them:

1. Salt

Salt is a highly strong cleanser for heavier energies, and it may be used on crystals, stones, candles, and other items. You should double-check that the salt will not cause a chemical reaction that will harm the thing you are attempting to clean. Research may be required.

Overnight, bury your stones and crystals in a dish or basin of sea salt.

Bathe your instruments in warm salt water (caution: salt reactions can cause metals to corrode).

Place salt on your altar.

2. Moonshine/Sunshine

Light power can generate a lot of purifying energy. The sun's light is bright and intense, and its warmth and heat are beneficial to any tool. Simply leave your equipment in a safe spot outside during the day to burn out any undesired or accumulated energies.

The same can be done with Moonlight; it all depends on your goals. Because a full moon is the greatest time to cleanse your tools, you may need to time your purification around an Esbat. You might even use the full sun of the day and continue your cleansing through the full moon's night, bringing your tools back into your altar in the morning, giving them both the Sun and the Moon's purification energy (both masculine and feminine/ god and goddess energy).

3. Soil

Soil is extremely grounding and can transmute any energy it comes into contact with.

The Earth itself draws all of our energy, so if you can utilize it to clear and ground yourself, why not your tools?

Simply bury your equipment underground overnight to employ dirt as a cleansing and purifying agent. If you're concerned about your tools getting soiled, wrap them in a cloth first, then set them in the soil, covering them completely. In the morning, dig them out and return them to your altar with a blessing.

4. Smudging/Incense

When the first three solutions aren't advisable or convenient, use incense or smudge sticks to cleanse your gear.

Smoke expels a lot of energy, especially when combined with plants used for cleansing. White Sage is a common choice, although other herbs, such as rosemary lavender, can also be used.

You only need to let the smoke cover your tools. You can either wave your tool through the smoke or waft the smudge stick or incense over it. It is also an excellent method for cleansing and refreshing the energy of the entire altar, which is difficult to bury in salt or dirt or transport outdoors into the sun and moonlight.

Charge Your Altar Tools and Implements in Step 4

After cleansing the energy of the altar and your tools, you can now charge them with the energy you require, such as whatever your spell's aim is. You may also wish to charge the energy of the altar and the tools to assist them in resting comfortably between rituals and spell casting after they have been cleansed and before returning them to their positions on the altar.

You may imbue your intentions into almost any tool. The intention is the key, and focus is the key to setting an intention within your tools.

Here are some suggestions for charging your instruments after they've been purified:

Step 1: Simply hold it in your hand and send intention energy into it.

This may not sound particularly magical, but it is! We are pure energy, and comprehending that concept is an important component of Wicca. When you hold something in your hand, like a quartz crystal, and desire to charge it with the energy of clarity and concentrated divination, you are telling the energy of that crystal, with your energy, what you want it to carry. That energy will then be available to you whenever you summon the stone.

You can do the same with a candle that will be used in a spell, charging it in your hand with your powerful intentions and asking it to receive the energy of what you are attempting to materialize.

You are lighting the energy of your intentions when you light the candle.

Sunlight and Moonlight, Step 2 Again

You've seen how sunlight and moonlight can both cleanse and purify your tools. They may, however, charge them with their strong energy. As the expression goes, you can kill two birds with one stone.

goes, by using the sun's/energy moon to both cleanse and charge whatever equipment you're working with.

The main thing is to be explicit about how you want your equipment to be charged. One effective method is to write your purpose on paper and then place the tools on top of that paper in the sun/moonlight loud as you lay out the tools, requesting that when the energy clears from them, they be filled with [insert intention or magical purpose here].

You get the idea. The sun and moon function in both directions as long as your manifestation intentions are clear.

Step 3: Charge Your Tools with Other Tools

Depending on the nature of the ritual or spell, you may end up charging the energy of another with several objects from your altar. You may not need to charge all of them at the same time, so utilize your available tools to boost strength and focus on your intention setting and charging routine.

One idea would be to place a pentacle slab in the sun and place whatever tool you want to charge on top of it. Set your intention and allow the pentacle's already existent power to infuse extra energy into your equipment. Another example is aiming your wand or athame at the tool to be charged while invoking or incanting some powerful words into it.

This is a very direct and targeted method of charging your tools. The employment of other tools will always add more energy and power to something, as long as the goal is there.

Step 4: Visualization is Critical

Set intentions and charge your tools and altar with your third eye. Wicca honors your psychic sense as well as your ability to connect to your higher knowing and higher sight.

When working with your instruments and altar, you can charge them by using creative imagination in your mind's eye.

Consider what you want your equipment to have in terms of energy.

Imagine what that could seem like in your thoughts. Assume you're attempting to charge a stone or crystal with healing energy.

Close your eyes and visualize a healing color, whatever colors you are (gold, green, and turquoise are common). Imagine a bright light of that hue radiating from the stone as you speak words to charge it, or simply holding it in your palm while seeing a multicolored light mandating from it.

Visualization, when combined with other charging stages, can make a significant difference in the amount of energy you put into your magical things.

Step 5: Make Use of Your Words

Words matter and the words you use are a crucial component of your overall practice and how you produce magic. It doesn't have to be elaborate while charging your tools. It can be as easy as this:

I charge this [name the item or object] with divine power to bring [name the magical intention] into my life.

As a result, it is!

If you want to get a little fancier, go ahead and do so. The more detailed you are, the better, and so many of Wicca's spell casting and ritual terms are like small poems and melodies. Have fun and don't be afraid to rhyme:

On this third day of June, by the light of the moon, I bring this object to light.

I say a big prayer, offering the message of sight restoration through the air.

Allow this crystal to appear whenever I am nearby and reveal more of my dreams to me.

I let a diviner's stone shine on me.

By the moon, so mote it be!

Step 6: Consecrating Your Tools for Your Altar

Consecration of your tools usually goes hand in hand with your charging of them, but you don't have to do this if you are not ready to invoke deities or external energies from outside of yourself.

Typically, consecration is a bit more elaborate and may involve more, or all of your tools. You will want to invoke your deity of choice for this and will also likely want to cast a circle for the experience.

It may seem like a lot of effort, but when you experience the energy that results from this powerful cleansing, charging, and consecration, you will understand right away. Try doing a spell without cleansing, charging, and/or consecrating your tools, and then try it again after you do. Notice the difference, and you will notice just how powerful these energies truly are.

In the next chapter, you will get more acquainted with your Wicca Starter Kit's guide to casting a circle. Now that you have your tools and your altar all set up, the next big step is casting the energy circle and calling in the elements and the deities. It is the basics of spell casting and ritual in Wicca. and lavender.

You only need to let the smoke cover your tools. You can either wave your tool through the smoke or waft the smudge stick or incense over it. It is also an excellent method for cleansing and refreshing the energy of the entire altar, which is difficult to bury in salt or dirt or transport outdoors into the sun and moonlight.

Charge Your Altar Tools and Implements in Step 4

After cleansing the energy of the altar and your tools, you can now charge them with the energy you require, such as whatever your spell's aim is. You may also wish to charge the energy of the altar and the tools to assist them in resting comfortably between rituals and spell casting after they have been cleansed and before returning them to their positions on the altar.

You may imbue your intentions into almost any tool. The intention is the key, and focus is the key to setting an intention within your tools.

Here are some suggestions for charging your instruments after they've been purified:

Step 1: Simply hold it in your hand and send intention energy into it.

This may not sound particularly magical, but it is! We are pure energy, and comprehending that concept is an important component of Wicca. When you hold something in your hand, like a quartz crystal, and desire to charge it with the energy of clarity and concentrated divination, you are telling the energy of that crystal, with your energy, what you want it to carry. That energy will then be available to you whenever you summon the stone.

You can do the same with a candle that will be used in a spell, charging it in your hand with your powerful intentions and asking it to receive the energy of what you are attempting to materialize.

You are lighting the energy of your intentions when you light the candle.

Sunlight and Moonlight, Step 2 Again

You've seen how sunlight and moonlight can both cleanse and purify your tools. They may, however, charge them with their strong energy. As the expression goes, you can kill two birds with one stone.

goes, by using the sun's/energy moon to both cleanse and charge whatever equipment you're working with.

The main thing is to be explicit about how you want your equipment to be charged. One effective method is to write your purpose on paper and then place the tools on top of that paper in the sun/moonlight speak it aloud as you lay out the tools, requesting that when the energy clears from them, they be filled with [insert intention or magical purpose here].

You get the idea. The sun and moon function in both directions as long as your manifestation intentions are clear.

Step 3: Charge Your Tools with Other Tools

Depending on the nature of the ritual or spell, you may end up charging the energy of another with several objects from your altar. You may not need to charge all of them at the same time, so utilitylike of your available tools to boost strength and focus on your intention setting and charging routine.

One idea would be to place a pentacle slab in the sun and place whatever tool you want to charge on top of it. Set your intention and allow the pentacle's already existent power to infuse extra energy into your equipment. Another example is aiming your wand or athame at the tool to be charged while invoking or incanting some powerful words into it.

This is a very direct and targeted method of charging your tools. The employment of other tools will always add more energy and power to something, as long as the goal is there.

Step 4: Visualization is Critical

Set intentions and charge your tools and altar with your third eye. Wicca honors your psychic sense as well as your ability to connect to your higher knowing and higher sight.

When working with your instruments and altar, you can charge them by using creative imagination in your mind's eye.

Consider what you want your equipment to have in terms of energy.

Imagine what that could seem like in your thoughts. Assume you're attempting to charge a stone or crystal with healing energy.

Close your eyes and visualize a healing color, whatever that color is for you (gold, green, and turquoise are common). Imagine a bright light of that hue radiating from the stone as you speak words to charge it, or simply holding it in your palm while seeing a multi-colored light emanating from it.

Visualization, when combined with other charging stages, can make a significant difference in the amount of energy you put into your magical things.

Step 5: Make Use of Your Words

Words matter and the words you use are a crucial component of your overall practice and how you produce magic. It doesn't have to be elaborate while charging your tools. It can be as easy as this:

Chapter 4

How to Cast a Circle Step by Step

In Wicca, casting a circle is like putting butter on your bread. It's the

The opening moment for you to connect with your ritual, spell, or prayer, and while working with the produces a focused goal of protection divine forces You can invent your variation of circle casting based on what you have read thus far, but as a Starter Kit Guide, this chapter will walk you through the process of opening a basic circle for short and simple tasks, as well as a more sophisticated, formal circle that will rely on my strength and require a little more time and effort

The components of the basic circle and the ritual circle are the same. The most significant part is the recognition and summoning of the four directions. The Elements, as you have seen throughout this book, are magical tools, and each one corresponds to a cardinal direction. When you ask for instructions, you are also asking for help. On the Elements and start a more focused magical practice with these energies available to you

Another important thing to remember is that your circle is supposed to be a shield of defense against harmful energies When you open it, you can open yourself to the divine by opening yourself to several different possibilities.

As a result, your circle of magic serves as a protective shield against these forces. keep you safe while performing your rituals You may choose to conduct more elaborate things while working with magic at first, utilize circle casting, and subsequently on to simpler forms later on, as you gain confidence in your abilities. Take a look at these straightforward, step-by-step casting instructions.

Bring in your selected tools as well as your altar for extra strength.

Circle Casting Fundamentals

Step 1: Where Will It Be Located?

Choosing where to throw your circle is determined by what

What are your goals? You may be performing some cooking magic with your cooking; therefore, your circle would just need to include the area where you cook. You may alternatively only require the space in front of your altar to perform your ritual.

Say a blessing or a prayer, and that's all there is to it. For a straightforward and fundamental All you have to select is where you will be casting performing your craft and the amount of room you may require If you won't need a large one if you're standing in one position the entire time.

Before you cast, think about where you're going to cast it.

Step 2: What Do I Require?

To cast a simple circle, you only need yourself. It might be as simple as placing your finger on the floor and determining north, moving in a circular circle, and speaking in each direction You don't need all of your instruments, candles, and incense. You can just set your intentions using the strength of your energy. Then simply point out the directions with your hands, fingers, and eyes.

You may require a compass, in general, assist to u guide yourself in the right direction. as you walk around the circle in the appropriate direction

Step 3: How to Start

Use your imaginative visualizing talents when casting your circle.

Visualize a protective shield surrounding you. It may appear to be a

Whatever works best for you, whether it's a glass orb or a blanket of white light.

1. Begin by pointing your finger northward, either on the floor or directly in front of you, as in "I invoke the forces of the North and the Earth element to defend and protect me as I travel

"I am receptive to the divine powers of everything."

2. In a clockwise direction, identify the East and say the

"I invoke the powers of the East and the West," he says air element to protect and guard me as I open to the divine

 all-powerful beings."

3. In a clockwise direction, identify the South and say the

"I appeal to the powers of the South and the West," he says.

fire element to guard and protect me as I open to the divine all-powerful beings."

4. In a clockwise direction, identify the West and say the

"I appeal to the powers of the West and the East," he says.

water element to defend and protect me while I open to the all-powerful celestial powers."

5. Returning to your initial spot, you can place your palms together in a praying stance, or extend your palms to receive While summoning the fifth element, you will receive divine energy.

"I call on the energy of the universe," said Spirit.

Great Mother and Universe, please help me with my magic.

6. You can modify the wording whatever you want, or simply leave them as is.

sense and consider the meaning of these phrases You are not required to mention anything.

To cast, they must be spoken aloud. It all comes down to intent.

7. Experiment with your intended magic!

Step 4: How to Finish

1. Beginning in the West position, where you finished the opening Point your finger on the floor or directly in the center of your circle.

"I thank the powers of the West and the East," he says in front of you. Water is your protector and guardian element. And so, it is."

2. Find the South saying by turning counterclockwise "I am grateful to the powers of the South and the for your protection and care, use the element of Fire.

3. Locate the East saying by moving counterclockwise.

"I thank the powers of the East and the West," he said.

air element for your protection and guardianship

4. Locate the North saying by moving counterclockwise.

"I thank the powers of the North and the powers of the South," he said.

Earth element for your protection and guardianship

5. Returning to your initial spot, you can place your palms together in a praying stance, or extend your palms to receive While summoning the fifth element, you will receive divine energy.

Spirit, with the words: "I give thanks to the divine for assisting me on my magical mission That is correct! " Closing your circle is similar to opening it, except that you begin from the West and return counterclockwise to the north, finishing with thanks to any spiritual life force deities you invoke to assist you with your magical requirements

Casting a Ritual Circle

Casting large for a more intricate experience incorporating ceremonies. A ritual circle is a more formal way of casting spells or commemorating Sabbats and Esbats' comprehensive method and envisioned a more powerful energy opening as well as other tools and setup

It's a lot of fun to turn your magic into a bigger event wishing to perform and so having access to all of your tools and resources. Making a larger casting experience will allow you to connect with more people. profoundly to your heavenly power and spiritual qualities. You won't need many decorations or intricate arrangements planning. You will only need your altar and the tools you already have set up. There are numerous approaches to this procedure, and, as such, with any other type of Wiccan magic, your imagination is always welcome.

Step 1: Where Will It Be Located?

As with your Basic Circle Casting, select the appropriate space as the first step to identifying your requirements. You may make a more elaborate circle needing o do a lot more movement and planning within your circle, therefore it should be large enough for you to dance around, or relocate to a variety of locations. If you are working outside, you must establish the perimeter of where you must cast For an outdoor celebration, such as a Sabbat or a wedding, an Esbat, these types of circles may require additional instruments and preparations.

You will frequently want your altar to be a part of your ritual practice finding a means to cast with your altar in the middle or at a distance Depending on what you want, a point of importance in your circle can be ideal. You have fantastic goals.

Step 2: What Do I Require?

For a ritual circle casting, you should use more of your tools such as, but not limited to with relation to the following:

The earth element, such as a bowl of salt or soil; pentacle

Air elements, such as incense and feathers, or any other object may represent Air

Candles and athame are examples of fire elements.

A chalice or a bowl filled with water is an example of a water element.

Wand

Stones and crystals for your circle (optional)

lighters and matches

Compass (optional)

Salt (optional)

Seating chair or pillow (optional)

All of these tools can be changed with whatever feels significant to you.

to you and appropriate for your ritual purposes in general, when it comes to casting a

You should include an abject, or numerous objects, in a larger circle. Objects in the four cardinal directions' spaces as you refer to each You can place the things in their designated locations by directing them into your point of the circle, exposing yourself and your magic to greater scrutiny and increased authority

As an example, place your athame at the southernmost point of your body.

Before proceeding to the West, form a circle and light a candle or two for your chalice and/or water dish

You can start with a compass, but as you get better at it, you may ditch it. You will always know where North is if you practice in your environment. Some witches will place stones and crystals in the center of the circle, each cardinal direction to create a more potent energy force field You can also use salt if you are comfortable with it.

Sweeping it up after you've completed your circle It is customary to pour salt in rounds a wonderful method to protect your energy and build on your circle. This instrument can even be used in your Basic Circle Casting Ritual. You simply cast your circle with salt, reciting the names of the directions and requesting protection. If you need a chair or a pillow to sit on while performing spells and rituals,

Before you start, make sure they are inside your circle cast. Additionally, ensure that all of the tools you require are contained within the Before you cast, make a circle. You don't want to have to cut the circular in half to dash to the kitchen and get some herbs Prepare yourself and Set it up with all of the supplies and tools you'll need to work on your magic

Step 3: How to Start

1. Place yourself in the center of your planned circle and three times, inhale deeply and expel completely. This is a solid foundation act to focus your attention and open you up to

the energy of intentions for casting. It's essentially a meditation to get you ready for magic.

2. To point at anything, you can use a wand or your pointer finger to the location on the floor where you know the North is, and the size of your circle (for example, if you're building a larger circle, you must point farther away from yourself that northernmost point).

**NOTE: Some Wiccans begin with the East and work their way north.

Position themselves as the last to call into the circle. It is entirely up to you whether or not

Depending on your preferences, you can begin or end with North.

Imagine a figure of protection as you point to the north. It could be a deity, or simply a hooded warrior or cloaked person who will bring Protection and light energy Consider them your Northern protectors. Recognize their presence by bowing your head. Make use of a few words to invoke their protection, such as "I invoke the Guardian and North's protector and Earth's element should keep an eye on this "Magical circle." You can also place your Northern goods and equipment in this area.

The location now, or set them up ahead of time if you already have wanted your circle's cardinal directions to be ready before you Take your three deep breaths from Step 1 and stand in the center.

3. Continue to move your wand/pointer finger

In this example, it is the next cardinal direction, traveling counterclockwise, If you start with the North, your destination would be the East.

first position Step 2 should be repeated to summon the East's protector. Consider their power and what they are capable of symbolizing or see your chosen god/goddess in this direction

4. Each time, repeat this method for the South and West imagining your Guardian and bowing your head. Once you have said the words of invitation

5. As you complete the circle and return to the starting point, North, visualize the circle drawn on the floor as well as the four guardians as protective towers

I charge this [name the item or object] with divine power to bring [name the magical intention] into my life.

If you want to get a little fancier, go ahead and do so. The more detailed you are, the better, and so many of Wicca's spell casting and ritual terms are like small poems and melodies. Have fun and don't be afraid to rhyme:

On this third day of June, by the light of the moon, I bring this object to light.

I say a big prayer, offering the message of sight restoration through the air.

Allow this crystal to appear whenever I am nearby and reveal more of my dreams to me. I let a diviner's stone shine on me.

By the moon, so mote it be!

Step 6: Consecrating Your Tools for Your Altar

Consecration of your tools usually goes hand in hand with your charging of them, but you don't have to do this if you are not ready to invoke deities or external energies from outside of yourself.

Typically, consecration is a bit more elaborate and may involve more, or all of your tools. You will want to invoke your deity of choice for this and will also likely want to cast a circle for the experience.

It may seem like a lot of effort, but when you experience the energy that results from this powerful cleansing, charging, and consecration, you will understand right away. Try doing a spell without cleansing, charging, and/or consecrating your too, l, a, and then try it again after you do. Notice the difference, and you will notice just how powerful these energies truly are.

In the next chapter, you will get more acquainted with your Wicca Starter Kit's guide to casting a circle. Now that you have your tools and your altar all set up, the next big step is casting the energy circle and calling in the elements and the deities. It is the basics of spell casting and ritual in Wicca.

6. Clasp your hands together and point both index fingers into the air, inviting the great spirit, God/goddess, deity, or Earth Mother to join you and defend you from above and around in your circle.

**

NOTE: Before you begin, you can draw a circle of salt on the floor to indicate where your circle will be and to offer an extra layer of protection. In addition to, or instead of, salt, you can place your tools or elemental objects at each cardinal point, and then add stones and crystals all around the circle's perimeter to designate the actual location you want to operate in.

This stage should be completed before you stand in the center and begin your incantations to call the directions. It is a far more orderly manner to form your circle.

You'll figure out what works best for you and build on it as you go, and with each sacred ceremony, you do.

Step 4: How to Finish

As with a Basic Circle, At the end of the ritual, it is critical to thank and release the energies that you have summoned for protection. This can simply mean repeating the opening circle, but this time working backward in a counterclockwise direction.

You can start where you left off in the opening, and if you are utilizing deities or images of guardians to defend your circle, make sure to thank each one as you walk back through your circle.

As a final offering, you might connect with the fifth element of spirit and express your gratitude for their participation in your rituals.

You can be as creative as you want with your incantations and closing words. If you have a candle lit for your southern position, now is the moment to extinguish it.

You can collect and replace any tools you used to connect with the cardinal directions on your altar. Depending on the type of

You may want to purify your equipment with incense or smudging at the end of any rituals you are doing. Return any crystals and stones to their proper places, and sweep up any herbs or salt.

Until your next circle casting, keep your altar neat. So, it shall be!

This step-by-step tutorial on casting a circle is a crucial component of your Wicca Starter Kit. As you have read, this form of magic will repeat itself over and over again, therefore it is critical that you become comfortable casting your circle of protection, no matter how simple or sophisticated it may be.

In the following chapter, you will be given some easy step-by-step instructions to assist you to understand the equipment and energies needed for a basic ceremony.

Chapter 5

Rituals: A Step-by-Step Guide

Rituals can take numerous shapes and signify many different things to a Wiccan or anyone who practices this type of magic.

Rituals have existed for as long as humans have existed, even in their most primitive forms. The ritual is a way for people to express their intents and devotions through the worlds of energy, elements, and spiritual connection, and as you will see in your studies, every civilization throughout history has some form of ritual practice.

Rituals in Wicca are about connecting with the divine, casting spells, making, and honoring the deities and cycles of life. They are unique to each practitioner or coven and can be offered in a variety of ways and styles.

The step-by-step guide to executing a ceremony will be included in your Wicca Starter Kit. Remember that each ritual must be updated and improved according to the magical objective you are working with. There may be numerous ingredients from which to choose work, as well as numerous phases and degrees, or levels, of practice that you must complete. It all depends on your spell and the steps you're doing with your Book of Shadows and solitary practice.

Many of the rituals done in a coven, or if you choose to join one, are already explained. This book is more focused on the ritual practices of a solitary Wiccan.

Let us begin with some fundamental and easy rules to assist you to visualize the process of your ritual activity.

Preparation is the first step.

Before you begin any ceremony, you must make the necessary preparations. All or part of the following preparations can be made:

The ritual's scheduling (Esbats and Sabbats have fixed dates.

Other ceremonies may require a specific date due to

Numerology, lunar and solar cycles, birthdays, and so on.)

Organizing the steps (You'll need to decide what sequence you need to carry out certain components of your ritual based on your knowledge of the spell you're working on or a reference to your Book of Shadows. Having the information readily available and in your cast, the circle is a vital aspect of the preparation process.) Gathering your materials (You will need a range of items for the ritual, not including your altar or standard tools. This can contain specific plants, crystals, candles, and colors, incense varieties, and so on.)

Bring all of your tools and ingredients into the space (You must have all of your collected tools, artifacts, ingredients, spell book, or ritual instructions, and anything else you may require in the space and ready to work on the specified day and time).

Setting boundaries with other aspects of your life (You will need to switch off your mobile phone and other distractions, as well as set a time and space with your family and loved ones to practice your ritual uninterrupted).

Other preparations may be found in addition to those on this list, depending on the precise ritual or spell you are attempting to cast.

Step 2: Forming a Circle

For every ritual you do, to maintain the sacred quality and nature of the experience, you will need to cast a Ritual Circle to support the energies you are attempting to engage with and focus on.

To prepare your circle of protection, follow the methods in Chapter 4 for Ritual Circle Casting. Check that all of your tools and supplies are in good working order. And that the objects you'll need for your ritual are already inside the area you'll be working in after you've cast your circle.

Step 3: Paying Respect to the Gods/Goddesses

One of the reasons people undertake rituals is to pay homage to a revered deity. Many Wiccans perform rituals for a certain God or Goddess regularly to help them enforce their energies to work on other magical reasons. The ceremonial honoring of a deity or spiritual presence is a sacred way to include that presence into your daily Wicca practice and will help tie you more firmly to the type of magic you choose to practice

Rituals open your space and energy to receive more of the divine presence's gifts, so after connecting to casting your circle of protection, you begin your words of blessing and prayer to the god or goddess you are calling into your ritual, either to honor them directly as the purpose of the ritual or to include them in whatever other ritual you are working to perform.

Step 4: Equipment and Ingredients

At this point in the ceremony, you will most likely require any necessary instruments and substances. You may have already used some of your instruments during the casting of your circle, so make sure to keep the equipment you need for your ritual instead of using them for circle placement. Instead of placing your water chalice in the west, set a bowl of water there and keep your chalice in the center with you or on the altar so that you can utilize it for your ritual.

Whatever herbs and ingredients you need to utilize can be prepared in whatever way you want. There will be particular directions for each ritual or spell, and you will need to have those instructions with you in the circle to prepare your herbs and essences correctly.

Your tools and ingredients will most likely be used in tandem to complement each other's energies. This stage of preparation might take place on your altar, a table, or the floor where you are sitting.

Step 5: Linking Your Intentions and Calling on Your Purpose

With your equipment and materials ready to use, you can begin the section of the ritual in which you change your tools and ingredients with the goals and purposes of the ritual you are conducting. In Chapter 3, you learned how to charge and consecrate your instruments.

You will imbue your ingredients, objects, and utensils with that sacred purpose at this step to prepare for the rest of the ceremony, depending on your spell work and objectives. Putting that magical intention into your items and tools first will only strengthen your ritual and is a necessary stage in the process. Be particular and clear in your intents and magical purposes, and allow your intentions and magical purposes to invoke the appropriate energy for the ceremony.

Step 6: Magic Practice

You can now begin practicing ritual magic with your charged and consecrated tools, implements, and materials. This stage will consist of a range of actions that will entirely depend on what your Book of Shadows suggests to do or what your spell work instructions may require of you. Some of these steps might be:

Lighting the candles for the spell (assuming you followed the previous step, they will already be charged, consecrated, and anointed).

Certain herbs are burned.

Invoking and honoring specific energies and/or deities by using your equipment in a specific way.

Dancing \Chanting \Speaking Words to spell

Pouring certain beverages into the chalice to sip while honoring a god or celebrating a festival

Appointing specific components to assist and guide you while you utilize your wand or athame.

In your cauldron, ingredients are being burned.

Other options will emerge as a result of certain rituals and spells. Some, none, or all of these things may occur during your ceremony, and it will be up to your Book of Shadows and intuition to construct the ritual and the procedures involved.

Step 7: The Influence of Words

This phase will largely overlap with Step 6, as the words you select for practicing magic will have a significant impact on your ritual.

You may speak words during ritual crafting and spell casting, but you may also speak words afterward to truly enhance and solidify your goals and purposes.

Your words are tailored to the occasion and can be as basic or as elaborate as you choose. A basic spell honoring the Triple Goddess on a Full Moon rite can use the following words:

I honor thee, Triple Goddess of the Moon, with the strength of three.

[when you light three candles, one for each element of the Goddess]

Maiden sweet of the spring moon, I'm lighting this candle in your honor.

[Bring out the maiden candle]

[Mother Candle]

I light this candle to commemorate you, Crone in the depths of the darker moon. [light

[the torch of the crone]

Sacred Goddess throughout the year, I worship you here on this full moon. [Fire your Triple Goddess plants to burn in your

cauldron]

Bring me your life force, birth-death-rebirth, under the light of the full moon. [fill your chalice with wine, water, or another liquid]

I raise my glass to thee, by the strength of three, to honor your divine wisdom. [Drink three drinks from the chalice, one for each facet of the Goddess.

the following three lines]

[sip] To the virgin

[sip] To the mother

[sip] To the crone

I honor your vision with this full moon.

So, it shall be!

Wicca is a creative discipline and a poetic expression of magical intent. Because your words have the ability to be crafted by your power, whatever you choose will especially strengthen your spells and rituals to assist you to gain deeper wisdom and a terrifying connection to the big divine. Before your ceremony, plan out the words you will speak and have them ready to read if you do not know them by memory.

Step 8: Complete Your Circle

After you have completed all of the procedures in the ritual, you begin to close the circle. Follow the same methods you taught in Chapter 4 for closing your circle and allowing your intentions to continue over into your life following your closing exercise. You can adorn your altar with any of your ritual materials, and you should reorganize your equipment on your altar so they are ready for the next ritual you prepare.

Following the Ritual

After you have returned your equipment and materials and closed your circle, you can now work with the energies you have summoned to assist you on your magical path. Your altar reminds you of the rituals you've done and why keeping your objectives alive and your attention pure.

Because the energy of your ritual can only endure so long, you must select when to proceed, cleansing your altar of any remnants of your previous ritual activity. As with other natural rhythms in life, you want to keep your energy flowing.

When the great energy of the ceremony has waned, use your intuition to discern when it is time to pass it forth into the next realm of spirit. You will know when you do more magic and delve into your inner direction throughout your practice.

Chapter 6

A Beginner's Guide to Spell craft and Basic Spells

There is an infinite supply of spells available online, in books, and through your friendships and relationships with other witches.

There is a whole business dedicated to spelling books, and people are working hard to offer more and more possibilities for making spells to make it all more accessible to practicing witches or Wiccan. There is no reason not to employ someone else's spells, but this book encourages a more creative approach and recognizes the gift of constructing your spells for your own goals. Spells, like you, adapt and change, and it is fine to experiment and be creative. To help you write and organize your spells, there are a few easy principles and step-by-step instructions. This chapter will provide you with the framework you'll need to get started on your Book of Shadows by practicing your creative magic and spell writing.

Writing Your Spells: A Step-by-Step Guide

Step 1: Figure out what your goal, intention, or magical purpose is.

The aim or purpose is what will help you structure everything about your spell, and it is possibly the most crucial phase in constructing it. What are you hoping to achieve? Do you want to find love?

Do you want to attract more financial abundance and prosperity into your life? Do you want to pay homage to a specific deity?

There are numerous choices, each of which necessitates a specific goal. Make your point. Be straightforward. Maintain simplicity. Know exactly what you want to magically produce honestly and directly so that you can build and create your spell around that purpose.

Step 2: Determine what you will require to achieve your goal.

Spells require tools and supplies, though some may merely require a candle or a crystal. Whatever you require, you must first settle on a list of ingredients for your dish. Some of the elements will come from the list below, and all of them should be goal-specific based on your spell's intention:

Candles of various colors

Incense \ Herbs

Nature's Objects

Stones and/or crystals

Tools for the Altar

Containers, bowls, and mixing spoons (all consecrated for rituals)

Special clothing

Indoor or outdoor altar setup (spell specific)

You may find that you require even more elements than those listed here, and you may always add items to any spell that you construct dependent on the type of Wicca you practice and the type of spell you are casting.

Step 3: Establish a Timetable

Every spell requires distinct energy to direct it. Your spell may require a specified date or even a specific time of day.

You may require the entire sun to shine down on your spell, or the darkness and energy of a New Moon. Every spell has time to function, and that time can be at any time. Some spells will be ready to cast whenever you need them, and the outcomes may vary depending on your approach. strength of the spell, or generate a better probability of manifestation moment you choose to cast your spell is critical to the nature of your original purpose. Choose the timing based on your goals. If you wish to increase your wealth and security, you should cast your spell on a New Moon and keep an eye on your finances. increase in tandem with the Full Moon As a fresh start from the morning sunlight, you may require the vitality of the dawn hours to bring a highly focused day and job experience to fulfillment. All of your spells can be written down in the Book of Shadows you're creating, and it's a good idea to offer yourself feedback on the most powerful times to cast each spell. If you are repeating spells, you may need to experiment with the time of each spell to find the one that yields the best results for you.

Step 4: Choose Your Incantations and Words

Your words matter as you discovered in the previous chapter's Step-by-Step Guide for Rituals. They transport the meaning of your desire into the energy of the Universe to help it manifest, so be sure your wording and meaning are clear.

Writing your spell is an important aspect of the procedure and should always be done before casting your circle, not after. You must choose the correct words for your aim if you want your spell to work.

The world of magic isn't evil, but it may be amusing in terms of how you obtain your benefits and presents from spell labor. 'Be cautious what you wish for,' as the saying goes, and this is especially true when it comes to spelling casting.

Before you establish your objectives, make sure you know what you're asking for. It will almost certainly come back to haunt you.

Step 5: Arrange the Spell in a Usable Format

You are now ready to construct the spell after you have determined all of the ingredients from Steps 1-4. They are the puzzle parts, and you must now assemble the puzzle. This is the most enjoyable portion because it is the design phase of your spell.

You get to be the architect here, choose what happens first, next, and last. You will pick when to light the ceremonial candles and what words you will pronounce in conjunction with them. Lighting them is a sacred act. You will pick how you will include your herbs (burning, drinking as

A tea, exhibiting at the altar, wrapping for drying, and so on). You will choose when to pronounce the manifestation words in combination with each sacred and magical act.

Building the spell is a portion of the work you'll perform for your Book of Shadows. It serves as a journal for your writing spells and development, so don't be scared to scratch things out and modify certain features and factors. It is a work of art that is always evolving, just like every spell you make and every piece of magic you perform.

Step 6: Cast Spells

The finest part about creating a spell is using it. You will need to set aside time and space, as well as gather all of your components, to enjoy your work of magic art. Using your spells is the payoff and reward, and every time you use them, your aims and intents are set in motion.

The following part will provide you with some simple spells to help you get started and acquaint yourself with some basic spell examples.

Don't be afraid to take these spells and modify them to your desire.

Basic Spells to Help You Practice the Abundance Spell You will require:

If you can't find a solid copper bowl, substitute another metal, such as a silver goblet or chalice.

Three pieces of gold

Fresh spring water (you can also collect water from nature, such as a river, a waterfall, or a natural in

instruction

1. Schedule this spell to make use of the Full Moon's strength.

2. Make a sacred space at your altar and conduct your spell by candlelight at night. If possible, perform near a window so that you can benefit from the full moonlight streaming in.

You can also do this ritual outside to connect with the Full Moon energy.

3. Ensure that your environment is peaceful and that you are alone and undisturbed.

4. Half-fill the copper basin with spring water.

5. Form a Circle

6. Drop the gold coins in one by one.

7. Look for the moon's reflection in the water inside the bowl.

8. Concentrate on the reflection and say, "I pray that abundance pours into my life."

The light of the Full Moon awakens my wealth.

My goal is to be prosperous.

And my gratitude will remain from now till the end of time."

9. Complete your circle.

10. Set the bowl aside overnight. You can either leave it under the Full Moon or keep it on your altar.

11. Take the coins in the morning and place them in your handbag or wallet, being cautious not to spend them.

**NOTE: You can add herbs and other items, such as anointed candles representing money and abundance, to keep the fire safe.

overnight with your coin bowl

Attraction's Law Spell

What do you most need to attract in your life? Love?

Happiness? Wealth? Workplace advancement? Psychic perception? This spell can be used as a multi-purpose attraction spell for whatever your unique objective is. It is a spell that will assist you in empowering your energy to open to what you genuinely desire.

You will require:

There are two candles (color specific to intention)

Paper and pen (colored pens can be used to emphasize your intention)

lighter/cauldron matches

1. You can use your altar place or another location where you can focus and be alone.

2. Make sure you're in the correct frame of mind to cast this spell.

Any negative or skeptical thoughts you have will have a detrimental impact on the energy of your spell.

3. Make a Simple Circle

4. Write down your intentions on paper. Be specific and concise.

5. Put out your candles.

6. If you want, read your intentions aloud.

7. Set fire to the paper with the flames of both candles.

8. Burn the paper in your cauldron carefully.

9. While the paper is burning, repeat the following words as many times as you can before it burns completely: "Let me be seen, heard, and blessed on this day, harming no one on my route."Close your circle before moving on to the next step.

11. Take your cauldron outside and either feed the ashes to the wind or let them fall from the pot and drift into the air.

12. Instead of blowing out your candles, snuff them out or leave them burning.

13. Repeat this spell up to nine times in a row to increase the potency.

14. If you aren't seeing any effects after a month, clear your energy and objectives and try again.

Spell of Herbal Love Charm

This spell is a charm that will help you release your blockages to love so that you can better attract it into your life. A sachet of herbs fashioned into a charm is an excellent approach to increase your receptivity to love. It's fine if you can't get all of the herbs on the list! Simply work with what you can find. You will require:

5-8 whole garlic cloves

1 teaspoon mugwort (dried)

1 teaspoon lemon balm (dried or fresh)

1 tablespoon St. John's wort (dried)

Chamomile flowers, 1/3 cup (dried)

3 tablespoons rose petals (dried or fresh)

bowl

1 light pink candle

a square piece of linen and string to make a sachet (similar to a potpourri bag)

Instructions:

1. Form a Circle (basic or ritual)

2. Prepare your ingredients for use on your altar.

3. Light your candle while taking deep breaths and contemplating your intentions.

4. In a mixing basin, combine the chamomile, mugwort, lemon balm, and St. John's wort using your fingers.

5. Pour the contents onto the cloth.

6. Garnish with rose petals and cloves.

7. Tie the cord around the sachet.

8. Hold the love charm in your hands in front of the candle and imagine your entire body is covered in white light from the inside out.

Consider it gushing from your heart and filling your entire existence.

It can even fill the entire circle you've created.

9. Now, as you hold your charm, let beautiful, pink light pour from your heart into the white light.

10. Repeat three times the following phrase, or whatever feels right to you:

"With this charm of loving herbs, I shall disturb my blockages to love, removing them from my life, awakening love and bringing light."

Play with the words to get the best meaning for you. The spell is about removing any impediments to allowing love to flow freely through you and accepting it honestly.

11. Allow the candle to burn on its own (make sure it is in a safe place to burn for an extended period).

12. Draw a circle around yourself.

13. Wear your charm and keep it close to you as much as possible. Even sleep with it beneath your pillow.

14. Once the charm has served its purpose, you can bury it in the ground or sprinkle the herbs somewhere, such as in a running river, to allow your love to flow or grow.

Chapter 7

Crystal Magic: A Step-by-Step Guide

Crystals are a common instrument for sharing and boosting energy. They're great for carrying around, holding in your hand, or wearing as jewelry. Most Wiccans utilize crystals and stones regularly because of how strong their energy is naturally and how easily they absorb the type of energy you want to take with you when you charge and consecrate them.

There are numerous crystals and stones available for purchase for use in rituals, and when you utilize these tools, they will follow the same basic principles as your other instruments:

They must be cleaned regularly.

They can be charged and sanctified as many times as needed.

They will accumulate unwanted energy over time, so cultivate a relationship and intuition with these items.

Respect their energy and power by keeping them in sacred areas.

If you already have certain stones, you may be aware that each one has its personality and quality. Some stones are specifically for protection, as well as stones that attract riches and fortune. Some are ideal for grounding, while others are best for developing clear channels of connection with your life or with the divine.

Here are a few crystals and stones you might be working with to help you with your solitary practice:

Amethyst: purple crystal- self-discipline, pride, sobriety, inner strength, calm fears or anxieties, open dreams and psychic visions, clear channel for contact with the spirit, aids in the breaking of habits and addictions

Black Tourmaline purifies auras, breaks obsessions, relieves anxiety, repels negativity, and protects the spiritual plane from psychic attacks. Shielding protection and grounding

Black Onyx is a hard, black stone that is used for banishing and releasing. Negativity and conflict wards Stone of protection. Increases confidence and strength.

Blue Kyanite is a crystalline-blue stone that promotes clear personal truth, fresh chapters, and the clearing of auras and chakras. Unlike other stones, it does not need to be cleansed or purified.

Carnelian is a vivid orange stone that represents passion, drive, courage, inspiration, personality, success, inner fire, goal manifestation, productivity, directness, joy, warmth, and illumination.

Citrine is a cheerful yellow crystal that represents the sun, joy, warmth, friendship, communication, dream manifestation, and individualism.

Hematite is a powerfully magnetic mineral that can be used for all types of attraction magic, protection, stability, grounding, clear comprehension, and perspective.

Lapis Lazuli: a deep blue with sparkles of gleaming pyrite- openness, insight, honesty, inner power, spiritual universal truth, intuitive thinking interpretation, psychic ability, soul guide magic

Moonstone: milky white/grey – moon magic, intuition, life cycles, empathy and clairvoyance, emotional love, heart connections, empathy and compassion Quartz Crystal: clear and glassy- all-purpose energy stone, personal strength, and energy, clearing, balance, healing, spiritual growth and enlightenment, objectives amplified. Rose Quartz: a gentle pale pink stone that promotes compassion, tolerance, love, and peace, as well as revealing inner beauty, self-confidence, partnerships, and self-love.

Tiger's Eye: warm golden brown courage, willpower, loyalty, truth, luck, protection, truth-seeking, perception, penetrates illusions, exposes manipulative or dishonest motives.

Turquoise: vivid blue with dark veining- master healer stone, inner beauty, joy, relaxation, healing, contentment, positive vibrations, prosperity, joy, friendship, protection, negativity neutralization, empath stone

Crystal Magic Step-by-Step Instructions

Your intentions and energy, like everything else you've studied in this Wicca Starter Kit, are what cast magic. You can now charge and consecrate all of the tools you collected in your tool kit, as well as use them for certain spells and rituals.

Crystals have numerous applications, and you will learn more about what they can do and how they can improve and enhance your magical spells as time goes on.

This basic step-by-step guide will explain to you how to care for and use your crystals and stones. They will work for you if you look after their energy.

Clear and Charge is the first step.

The first step in working with any crystal is to ensure that it has been cleaned.

They are incredibly absorbent and can contain a lot of energy, more than you might think when you hold them in your hands.

The step-by-step instructions for cleansing your crystals and stones can be found in Chapter 3: Step 3. The same restrictions apply to all of your tools, including your crystals.

You can use salt, soil, sunlight, moonlight, or smoke.

Regular cleansing of your stones is critical to the magic you practice.

The next best thing you can do is charge your stones. These processes are also covered in Chapter 3: **Step 3,** and you can charge in any way you see fit. The secret to basic stone and crystal charging is to use your energy to imbue them with your tremendous essence and magic. Set the intention for your stones to be clear, full of loving light, and imbued with the power of the universe whatever source you choose to use: sun, moon, fire, smoke, etc.

Step 2: Perform the Magic

You now have all of the steps you need to cast the correct kind of magic with your stones, thanks to your new knowledge of rituals and spell casting from chapters 5 and 6. Once your stones have been charged, you can cast magic with them and keep them energetically present throughout the spell's activity.

You can either leave them on the altar or bring them with you. Casting the magic is the process of putting your intentions and magical purpose into stone. The crystals absorb your magical intention and become filled with your purpose and needs.

Consider casting a basic or ritual circle and writing a spell specifically for using crystals so that you can put the power and force of your spell work into these powerful conduits of energy and spirit.

Step 3: Access the Crystals' Energy

When the spell is finished, you can use the energy collected in the crystal to carry it with you. Depending on your wants and uses, you may want to use your stone to guard your automobile and put it on the dashboard; you may want to encourage your garden to grow healthy and full, so you will plant several of them in your garden bed, or you may need it under your pillow to inspire lucid dreams.

Whatever the spell requires, you must now harness the power of the magic housed in your crystal and call on it regularly to create your magic work.

4th Step: Clear and Charge

Your spell's power and might will eventually fade, as will the energy in the stone. After reaping the advantages of your crystal spell, you will return to the first stage by cleansing and charging your crystal for its next magical usage.

If you're dealing with crystal magic, these procedures are essential to ensuring that you get the most out of the energy of crystals and stones. Have fun with it, and here's crystal magic to get you started:

Clear Communication with a Crystal Spell

Use this charm to strengthen communication at home, at business, or even with the divine or favored deities.

Charging a stone or a crystal with your magical goal and purpose is a very effective technique to open yourself to that magic.

As previously said, stones and crystals are extremely powerful and contain a great deal of energy. This spell is an excellent approach to infuse the power of your goals into your stone or crystal. It is intended to be carried or worn on the person to connect to the energy of that purpose throughout the day.

Aquamarine, amethyst, and clear quartz are required (optional)

1 yellow or white candle (colors of communication)

Because aquamarine connects the heart and throat chakras, it creates a clean channel of heartfelt, honest, open, and compassionate communication. This is a stone for telling the truth.

You can also augment that power by carrying a piece of lapis lazuli with you (optional).

Amethyst is known for expanding your senses to divine and spiritual connections. It can eliminate energy blockages and improve energy flow, including communication.

When combined with the other elements, quartz can be used to increase the overall potency of your spell.

1. Begin by drawing a basic circle.

2. Light your candle and place your amethyst (and quartz) in front of it.

3. Place your aquamarine (and any extra stones) in both hands, and palms together.

Close your eyes and center yourself. Take a few deep breaths.

5. Spend some time imagining your communication moment, as well as the relaxation and joy you feel as a result of your clear and straightforward communication. Consider how amazing it feels to express yourself calmly and openly.

6. Visualize the energy flowing from you into the stone through your hands.

7. Speak the following sentences while holding the stones: My voice is true and clear, from the heart.

I give these stones my powerful start, using my clear as a bell voice to convey my truth and everything I have to say."

That is correct!

**NOTE: If you desire to speak with the divine rather than a family member or boss, adjust the language you use to reflect that goal and aim.

8. Now, set the aquamarine (and/or other stones) next to the amethyst and quartz and allow the candle to burn for at least an hour, or until it is completely consumed.

9. Complete your circle.

10. You can now carry your stone with you to provide the energy of clear communication when you need it the most.

You can also add herbs and oils to your candle to give this spell even more power and magic. Frankincense essential oil and dried peppermint are fantastic ways to improve the clarity of your candle's magic message.

Chapter 8

Candle Magic: A Step-by-Step Guide

Candle Magic is simple and enjoyable. A candle is one of the most critical items you'll need for any spell you cast. It not only represents the element of fire and the direction of the south, but it also adds light to your altar and life power to your spells. As you can see in Chapter 2, it is the only tool in the tool kit that can represent all of the elements.

All you need to know about candle magic are a few fundamentals:

1. Colors- each color in the rainbow has a mystical meaning. The color of the candle you use has a significant impact on your spell. Each hue has a different meaning, and you may need a range of colored candles to trigger your magic. The hue has as much meaning as starting the flame.

2. Symbols- Symbols are frequently carved into the candle wax to give it greater power, purpose, and meaning.

Pentagrams and pentacles are common symbols, but you may already have a collection of symbols that you use for spells. Carving the sign into the candle and allowing it to melt away as the spell gathers power is a crucial aspect of the candle magic process.

3. Oils- rubbing oils over the sides of the candle adds another essence to the magic. The extra perfume may have a strong influence and positive output for your spell. Many Wiccans anoint candles with essential oils or even herbal olive oils for added magical emphasis. This is normally done before rubbing herbs over it.

4. Herbs- Herbs are often utilized in magic, and they can even assist you to consecrate your candles for increased magical power. Using dried or fresh herbs increases the potency of your spell by adding the potency of whatever you're using.

Because you want the herbs to attach to the edges of the candle, do this step after you've saturated it with oils.

Apply the procedures outlined above to your candle magic rituals to discover an even greater source of power in your craft work. Here is a list of candles' color meanings to assist you with your spells:

White represents purity, serenity, healing, truth and honesty, cleansing, spirituality, clarity, wholeness and joy, protection against negative energy, meditation, quiet, and focus.

Yellow represents intellect, inspiration and creativity, communication, confidence and charm, persuasion, wisdom, mental strength, and so on.

Personal power, self-esteem, cheerfulness, enthusiasm, and optimism are all characteristics of the Air element.

Orange is associated with success, joy, stimulation, energy, prosperity, good fortune, courage, energy building and boosting, power, legal matters, happiness and excitement, clearing negative emotions, attracting friendships, and emotional healing.

Pink represents all types of love, forgiveness, emotional and spiritual well-being, harmony, joy, compassion, and love spells.

Red represents fire and passion, fertility, sex, power, virility, potency, courage, blood, action, vigor, Mother (Triple Goddess), and the element of fire.

Purple represents spiritual awakening, vision, clairvoyance, inner eye, intuition, respect, honor, wisdom, purification, progress, spiritual growth, stress reduction, sleeplessness, and healing.

Blue represents soothing, inner peace, harmony, tranquility, patience, kindness, healing, serenity, truth, wisdom, communication, loyalty, and peaceful home.

Green represents Mother Earth, fertility, nature, growth, abundance, financial success, money, good fortune, prosperity, generosity, and mental and physical well-being.

Earth magic, Earth element, healing/rejuvenation, renewal, bountiful crop

Brown is associated with grounding, balance, earth vibration, clear thinking/decision-making, common sense, stability, material gain, focus, intuition, telepathy, finding lost objects, and animal healing.

Silver: neutralizes bad energies and effects, protects from entities, stabilizes, inner peace, and calm, and invokes female deities.

Gold is associated with sun gods and goddesses, attracting cosmic forces, riches, persuasion, victory, masculinity, confidence, and the invocation of male deities.

Black: dispels negativity, absorbs all colors, and is reversible hexes/curses repels dark magic, eliminates bad habits, resilience, self-control, inner strength, deeper consciousness, and healing help

Crone's loss and sadness (Triple Goddess).

Money Flow Candle Spell

This money attraction spell is designed exclusively for candle magic. It is critical that you trust that your intentions will be fulfilled and that you do not need to worry about how this will happen. The Universe will provide, and you must be open to all possibilities.

You will require:

a single candle (gold or green for money spells)

A candle holder or any surface that can be adhered to with melted wax (take safety precautions when working with candles)

Sewing pin or crystal (the point of the pin or crystal will be used to engrave a symbol into the candle)

Essential oil of patchouli (substitute olive oil if you have none) a pinch of dried basil

Patchouli and basil are herbs associated with prosperity and wealth.

You may come across additional herbs that provide the same type of magic, and you can choose different herbs if you find something you prefer.

Instructions:

1. Form a Fundamental or Ritual Circle

2. Inscribe a pentacle into the side of the candle with a pinpoint or crystal point (you can also choose other symbols related to abundance, such as runes or other ancient symbols if you choose).

3. Rub the patchouli oil on the sides of the candle to anoint it.

4. Roll the candle in the dry basil, allowing the herbs to adhere to the patchouli oil.

5. Insert your candle into its holder, making sure the symbol you etched on it is facing you.

6. Spend some time grounding yourself. Close your eyes and imagine yourself receiving money unexpectedly. You can also imagine yourself standing in a river of shiny coins and paper bills, with paper money raining down on you.

7. Speak the following lines, or something similar, while holding the vision in your mind: "With flaming light, I

summon divine energies; money comes to me from hidden sources."

Showering me with desired gifts, surprising my wallet with a boost!"

8. Light the light and say aloud, "So mote it be!" as the wick begins to burn.

9. Complete your circle.

10. Leave the candle lit until it burns out. Take appropriate safety precautions.

Conclusion

Congratulations! You have everything you need to get started on your journey as a single practitioner, casting spells and performing rituals. This book is a fantastic resource for you to use again and again as you create your toolbox of magical objects and practice casting spells with whatever you have available to you.

As you go, return to these pages as needed to assist you in writing your spells and rituals and determining the best methods for you to create space with your altar and instruments. Continue to seek out new information to supplement your magical practice, as well as new tools and implements of your creation or discovery to add to your rituals and toolbox.

I hope you found this book informative and helpful, and if so, a review on Amazon.com would be very appreciated. I'll leave you with some words to get you started, and may you discover all of the magic you need in these pages today!

May this road of light provide you with great wisdom as you proceed.

By the light of the Full Moon, I am casting magic and creating bright, ritual spells.

As you give birth to all the magic of your heart, honor Goddess, Mother Earth, and Father Sky, and may this book be your ideal start!

That is correct!